Birth of the Nation

*The creation of this book
and the exhibit with the same title
were funded by:*

New York State Commission on the Bicentennial
of the U.S. Constitution

United States Capitol Historical Society

Federal Bar Council

The William Nelson Cromwell Foundation

Publication sponsored by:

The Center for The Study of The American Constitution

Virginia Commission on the Bicentennial of the U.S. Constitution

The book and the exhibit were a joint project of:

First Federal Congress Project, The George Washington
University

The Second Circuit Committee on the Bicentennial of the
United States Constitution, New York, New York

Birth of the Nation:
The First Federal Congress
1789–1791

By Charlene Bangs Bickford
and Kenneth R. Bowling

Madison
House
PUBLISHERS, INC.

Madison 1989

Bickford and Bowling,
Birth of the Nation: The First Federal Congress, 1789-1791

LIBRARY OF CONGRESS CATALOGING-IN-PUBLICATION DATA

Bickford, Charlene Bangs.
  Birth of the nation.

  Includes bibliographical references and index.
  1. United States.   Congress (1st : 1789-1791)
2. United States—Politics and government—1789-1797.
I. Bowling, Kenneth R.   II. Title.
JK1059 1st.B53   1989b   328.73'09'033   89-14541
ISBN 0-945612-14-1

Printed on acid-free paper

Book designed by John DiRe/3000U

Cover: George Holland. *A View of Broad Street, Wall Street, and the City Hall.* Courtesy
of: I.N. Phelps Stokes Collection Miriam & Ira D. Wallach Division of Art, Prints and
Photographs. The New York Public Library, Astor, Lenox and Tilden Foundations

Published by

MADISON HOUSE PUBLISHERS, INC.
P.O. Box 3100
Madison, Wisconsin 53704

REVISED EDITION

Contents

Foreword   vii

Acknowledgments   ix

Sessions of the First Federal Congress   xi

Introduction   1

I   A New Beginning: Congress Convenes in New York City   9

II   Setting Precedent: Organizing Itself   15

III   An Imperial Presidency?   23

IV   The First Federal Revenues   29

V   Shaping the Executive Branch   37

VI   Defining the Federal Judiciary   45

VII   The Bill of Rights   51

VIII   Locating the United States Capital   55

IX   Funding the Revolutionary War Debt   61

X   The Compromise of 1790 and Its Reaffirmation in 1791   67

XI   "Westward the Course of Empire Takes Its Way"   77

XII   The Senate and Foreign Policy   87

XIII   Political Parties in the First Congress   93

Conclusion   99

Notes   101

Members of the Senate and House of Representatives   107

Index   111

Foreword

This publication, and the exhibit which it accompanies, are sponsored by the Second Circuit Committee on the Bicentennial of the United States Constitution, established in 1986 by the Honorable Wilfred Feinberg, then Chief Judge of the United States Court of Appeals for the Second Circuit, and chaired since that time by the Honorable James L. Oakes, the present Chief Judge, and the Honorable Lawrence W. Pierce, United States Circuit Judge.

The publication is made possible by a generous grant from the William Nelson Cromwell Foundation, to which the Committee wishes to express deep appreciation for its continuing support.

The exhibit which this publication accompanies will open in Washington, D.C. and at the United States Court House in Manhattan in the spring of 1989. Funding for the exhibit has been provided by the New York State Commission on the Bicentennial of the United States Constitution and the United States Capitol Historical Society, whose indispensable assistance the Committee gratefully acknowledges. The continuing participation of the Federal Bar Council in the historical activities of this Circuit is also greatly appreciated.

Special thanks are due to Charlene Bangs Bickford, Kenneth R. Bowling, Helen E. Veit and Katherine Reed Cavalcanti of the First Federal Congress Project at George Washington University of Washington, D.C. The authors of this publication and the creators of the exhibit, Mrs. Bickford and her associates have used their pre-eminent expertise to provide the first comprehensive presentation ever made of the work of the First Congress, a little-known but crucial event in our nation's history.

The Subcommittee on Commemorative Events
Second Circuit Committee on the Bicentennial of
the United States Constitution

Acknowledgments

The publication of this book provides us with the opportunity to recognize the contributions of the many individuals and institutions that have assisted with both the book and the exhibit by the same title.

The authors relied entirely upon the original sources available in the files of the First Federal Congress Project, where they are co-editors of the *Documentary History of the First Federal Congress, 1789–1791*, and Kenneth Bowling's research notes for his doctoral dissertation, Politics in the First Federal Congress, 1789–1791. First and foremost, we appreciate the continued and long term support for the First Federal Congress Project from the National Historical Publications and Records Commission and The George Washington University. In addition certain NHPRC staff members encouraged and assisted in this endeavor: Roger Bruns, Mary Giunta, Tim Connelly, and particularly Don Singer.

Our colleague, Associate Editor Helen E. Veit, read and edited the manuscript, improving it greatly through her substantive textual suggestions and her skilled editorial work. She served in the same capacity for the exhibit as well as participating in all other facets of that work, most notably serving as the "data organizer." Katherine Reed Cavalcanti proofread, transcribed, and generally assisted with any task involved with the exhibit and book.

To John D. Gordan III goes the credit for conceiving the idea of the exhibit, persisting in his commitment to it even when the chances for funding looked bleak indeed, and encouraging all of the major players, while making sure that deadlines were met. He truly deserves the title of "founding father" of this project.

We also gratefully acknowledge the generous support for this project from the judges of the Second Circuit, the Cromwell Foundation, the Foundation of the Federal Bar Council, the New York State Commission on the Bicentennial of the Constitution, and the United States Capitol Historical Society.

The designer of the exhibit, Heather McRae, worked patiently and creatively with scholars who had little experience with exhibits. She shaped an artistically pleasing exhibit without any sacrifice of historical integrity. John DiRe, the book's designer, accomplished his assignments with skill and rapidity which enabled the on-schedule publication.

While putting together the exhibit we were helped by numerous individuals and institutions. We gratefully acknowledge the courteous and able assistance from the following: Michael McReynolds, Joseph D. Schwarz, Ronald E. Swerczek, Mary Ryan, Angie L. Spicer, Terry D. Wallis, Judy Edelhoff, Catherine Nicholson, Mary L. Ritzenthaler, Bobby C. West, and Susan Amos, National Archives and Records Administration; Chuck Kelly, Mary Wolfskill, Clark Evans, Jim Gilreath, Rosemary Plakas, Robert Shields, Evelyn Nave, and Lee Carpenter, Library of Congress; Celeste Walker, Adams Family Papers at the Massachusetts Historical Society; Peter Drummey and Ross Urquhart, Massachusetts Historical Society; Audrey Milne, Dyer-York Library and Museum, Saco, Maine; Donald Eddy, Cornell University Library; Maine Historical Society; The New York Public Library; Richard Baker and Kathryn Jacob, Senate Historical Office; Raymond Smock, Historian, U.S. House of Representatives; Kim Baer, Pennsylvania Bar Association; Margaret Christman, National Portrait Gallery, Smithsonian Institution; Saundra Taylor, Lilly Library, Indiana University; John Catanzariti, *The Papers of Thomas Jefferson*, Princeton University; Jean Preston, Princeton University Library; the Fogg Art Museum, Harvard University; The National Gallery of Art; Charles Hobson, the *Papers of John Marshall*; Margaret Cook, Swem Library, College of William and Mary; Mary Giles, South Carolina Historical Society; Philip Cronewett, Dartmouth University Library; Mark Jones, Connecticut State Library; Cynthia Rom, Corcoran Gallery of Art; David C. Dutcher, Independence National Historical Park; Lois Long, Curator's Office, U.S. Supreme Court; Laura Monti and Roberta Zonghi, Boston Public Library; Cammie Naylor, the New-York Historical Society; Yale University Art Gallery; Jane Neale, the American Antiquarian Society; Arlene Shy, Clements Library, University of Michigan; George Talbot and Myrna Williamson, the State Historical Society of Wisconsin; Richard H. Kohn; George Curtis; Joan E. Hosteler and Douglas Clanin, the Indiana Historical Society; Carnegie Library of Pittsburgh; Richard Fyffe and Prudence Bachman, the Essex Institute; John Van Horne, the Library Company of Philadelphia; the New York Society Library; Barbara Sarudy and Jeff Goldman, the Maryland Historical Society; Linda McCurdy, William R. Perkins Library, Duke University; The Atwater Kent Museum; Chuck Rand and Butch Vasloh, The National Museum of American History, Smithsonian Institution; Gaspare J. Saladino and Charles Schoenlaeber, the Ratification of the Constitution Project, University of Wisconsin; and Richard Bernstein of the New York City Commission on the Bicentennial of the United States Constitution.

Charlene Bangs Bickford
Kenneth R. Bowling

Sessions of the First Federal Congress

FIRST SESSION

March 4 – September 29, 1789
New York City

SECOND SESSION

January 4 – August 12, 1790
New York City

THIRD SESSION

December 6, 1790 – March 3, 1791
Philadelphia

The federal ship Union, engraver unknown. *American Museum*, vol. IV
(Philadelphia, 1788). (Courtesy of the Library of Congress)

Our constitution, sir, is like a vessel just launched, and lying at the wharf, she is
untried, you can hardly discover any one of her properties; it is not known how she will
answer her helm, or lay her course; whether she will bear in safety the precious freight
to be deposited in her hold. But, in this state, will the prudent merchant attempt
alterations? Will he employ two thousand workmen to tear off the planking and take
asunder the frame? He certainly will not. Let us gentlemen, fit our vessel, set up her
masts, and expand her sails, and be guided by the experiment in our alterations. If she
sails upon an uneven keel, let us right her by adding weight where it is wanting. In
this way, we may remedy her defects to the satisfaction of all concerned; but if we
proceed now to make alterations, we may deface a beauty, or deform a well
proportioned piece of workmanship.

Speech by Representative James Jackson of Georgia, June 8, 1789. (*The
Congressional Register*, vol. I, page 416—Courtesy of the Library of Congress)

Introduction

In the present situation of America, and perhaps in almost every possible situation, it will be necessary for the government to follow, rather than to controul the general sentiment. The dissemination of just sentiments is not very difficult. The struggle to procure the adoption of the constitution, has sufficiently disposed the most influential men to the belief and propagation of the opinions most favourable to the government. If the imprudence of the government should not hurry them, by measures repugnant to these prepossessions, into the opposite system, I am in hopes that we shall think and act as a nation, and in proportion as state prejudices and preferences shall subside, the federal government will gain strength. (Rep. Fisher Ames of Massachusetts to William Tudor, April 25, 1789, Massachusetts Historical Society *Collections*, ser. 2, 8:317-18)

The First Federal Congress was the most important Congress in American history. Its awesome agenda breathed life into the Constitution, established precedent and constitutional interpretation which still guide us two hundred years later, and held the Union together when sectional interests threatened disunion and even civil war. Most significantly, it concluded the American Revolution.

The sense of closure was so clear that even contemporaries recognized it. In 1790 the historian Jeremy Belknap reported that the Bostonians planned a historical pillar to commemorate the American Revolution. It would list the most striking events, beginning with the Parliament's Stamp Act in 1765 and concluding with the First Federal Congress's Funding Act in 1790.

The American Revolution can be understood as a debate over federalism: before 1776 between advocates of the colonies on one side and of Great Britain, both Parliament and Crown, on the other; after 1776 between those who advocated the rights of the states and those who thought continentally.

The first act adopted by the First Federal Congress reflected the fundamental change of opinion which had occurred during the Revolution over the question of American federalism. The Oath Act implemented Article VI, paragraph 3 of the Constitution, which required that members of the state legislatures and all state executive and judicial officials take an oath to support the Constitution. Congress could have left implementation to the states, and some members expressed concern about ordering the states to do what they had already agreed to when they ratified the Constitution. Through a federal act Congress imposed a uniform oath and uniform standards for administering it. This was the opposite of what Anti-federalists had wanted. In fact, the New York Ratification Convention had gone so far as to propose as an amendment to the Constitution a requirement that all federal officials take an oath not to violate the rights of the states.

By 1774 many Americans had become convinced that their needs and opinions could not be heard in the British Parliament, even if some form of representation could be devised. Consequently, the First Continental Congress, meeting in the fall of that year, turned to the Crown for redress of American grievances. So too did the Second Continental Congress, which convened in the spring of 1775. The King ignored the petitions. Faced in 1776 by a central government deaf to their pleas and enforcing its silence with an army, Americans had to choose either independence or a constitutional status that left the central government supreme and the colonies without recourse.

In July 1776 Congress chose independence. It declared the fact to the world in an eloquent and bold declaration of impeachment against King George III. This new form of regicide, a constitutional statement severing all connection between the British Crown and the thirteen colonies, and the events which led up to it, profoundly affected the attitude of Americans toward the role of the executive in the United States.

At the same time as it appointed a committee to consider independence, Congress appointed another to consider a constitution which defined the relationship between the states and the United States in Congress assembled and between one state and another. The committee reported a draft on July 12, 1776, but the final document was not accepted by Congress until November 15, 1777.

On that day Congress submitted to the states the first United States constitution, the Articles of Confederation. In it the states were clearly supreme over Congress. Each retained its sovereignty, freedom, independence, and every power not *expressly* delegated to Congress by the Articles. Federal revenues consisted of apportioned requisitions on the states, based on land values in each, but Congress lacked the power to enforce their collection. Nor did it have the authority to regulate interstate commerce. There was no executive and only a primitive judiciary. But it was just the kind of constitution one would expect from political leaders who had been protesting against tyranny from the distant British Parliament and Crown.

To become effective, the Articles, as well as any subsequent amendments, had to be ratified by all thirteen states. The thirteenth did not ratify until February 1781. The Battle of Yorktown in October 1781 all but ended the War for Independence, a war which the United States had fought since 1775 without the benefit of a constitution.

From 1781 through 1788, the Articles of Confederation defined what the general government could and could not do. Even before ratification of the Articles, and especially after the war ended, several members of Congress sought to strengthen the general government at the expense of the states. Prominent among these were Alexander Hamilton of New York, James Madison of Virginia, and Oliver Ellsworth of Connecticut. They had the support of the two men to whom Congress had granted the greatest amount of executive authority: Commander in Chief of the Continental Army George Washington and Superintendent of Finance Robert Morris. By 1784, when Congress ratified the Treaty of Paris which recognized the independence of the United States, these men had concluded from repeated attempts that constitutional reform could not be accomplished within Congress. Retiring from the federal political arena, they turned to the press and private letters in an attempt to persuade the American people of the necessity of granting greater power to the general government.

In May 1787 a constitutional convention, a meeting for which these men and their allies had been campaigning since as early as 1780, convened in Philadelphia. Support for it came also from those who wished to rein in the growth of democracy within the states and those who saw a national economy as essential to meaningful economic growth. Relying on two centuries of political thought seeking a place for practical expression, more than a century of colonial and state experience, a twenty year public debate over the nature of American federalism, and the experience of a decade of central government, the Federal Convention proposed a new constitution for the United States.

Its most original contributions were the presidency and an amending process that did not require unanimity and allowed the Constitution to change over time, for the original intent was that the document be flexible enough to change with American society. As much as possible the Convention avoided any decision which might create enemies for the proposed Constitution; for example, it consciously chose not to grant Congress explicit power to charter banks, assume the state revolutionary war debts, or name the site of the federal capital city. Its decision not to flesh out the executive and judicial branches was related to the republican belief in legislative supremacy: Congress would have almost complete control over their structure and powers in 1789 and forever.

The Constitution resolved the question of American federalism by rejecting the views of those who called for a national or unitary government and the abolition of the states. Instead it retained the concept of a Union of states, but declared that the federal government was supreme over the states. And it endowed that government with the power of the purse and the power of the sword. In addition, it granted constitutional sanction to executive and judicial branches for the federal government.

Opposition to the Constitution arose immediately. Over the winter and spring of 1787–1788 Americans divided as they had not since 1774–1776. Federalists favored the Constitution as an essential step toward fulfilling the principles and

3

promises of the Revolution. Antifederalists opposed it as an over-reaction to the problems experienced under the Articles of Confederation and as inverting the federal equation by making the federal government supreme over the states. Both sides recognized that the decision at hand amounted to a second revolution. As one Federalist described the situation, "We are upon the Eve of another Revolution in the System of Government. . . . [It] leaves but the shadow of power in the States; utterly destroys the Old Ship, and a new one built, in which we must embark or sink."[1]

The Constitution became effective once nine states ratified it. The votes were close, especially in the large influential states, but eleven states had ratified by July 1788. The Confederation Congress took up the question of when and where the First Federal Congress would convene, when the presidential electors would be chosen, and when they would vote. All of these issues, except the meeting place of Congress, were resolved quickly.

Congress was divided between those who wanted to stay at New York City, the seat of government since 1785, and those who believed the First Federal Congress, like the First Continental Congress, should meet at Philadelphia. Other locations considered included Annapolis and Baltimore in Maryland, and Lancaster in Pennsylvania. After weeks of acrimonious debate, Congress finally agreed to an ordinance on September 13, 1788. Because of the bitterness of the fight, it did not name New York, saying instead, "the present Seat of Congress."

Immediately thereafter the first congressional election began. It had ended in most states by March 4, 1789, the date established by the Confederation Congress for the First Federal Congress to assemble. The last men to be elected from the eleven ratifying states, the New York senators, were chosen in July 1789. Senators were chosen by the state legislatures and reflected the influence of state political factions and parties. Representatives were chosen at large or from districts. The only issue to emerge as a national one was whether the Constitution should be amended.

Serious contests for seats in the House of Representatives arose in only fifteen of the forty-three districts: five of eight districts in Massachusetts, four of six in New York, one (Baltimore) of six in Maryland, four of ten in Virginia, one (Charleston) of five in South Carolina. Among the four states which chose their representatives at large, serious contests arose in Pennsylvania and New Jersey but not in Connecticut or New Hampshire. Despite early Federalist fears and an active campaign by Antifederalists in the larger states, Federalists swept to victory, electing twenty of twenty-two senators and forty-nine of fifty-nine representatives.

Three of the elections held particular significance for the work of the First Congress itself. After refusing to appoint James Madison to the Senate, the Virginia legislature forced him to run for the House in a heavily Antifederal district. He already had a national reputation and Americans throughout the country followed his campaign against his Antifederal friend James Monroe. Madison defeated Monroe, 1308 to 972.

The bitter personal contest in Charleston, South Carolina, between Federalists

William Loughton Smith and David Ramsay became the first contested election in the history of the House of Representatives. The House decided in favor of the victor, Smith, rejecting the argument in Ramsay's petition that Smith had not been a United States citizen for the seven years required by the Constitution.

The New Jersey congressional election also had to be reviewed by the House. Historically the state had been divided between the northern counties tied to New York City and the southern counties tied to Philadelphia. In the wake of the long congressional debate of 1788 over where the First Federal Congress should meet and expecting the new Congress to be confronted with the same issue, two tickets appeared which reflected the divided loyalties of the state. Accusations of fraud against both sides filled the five weeks of voting and electioneering, after which the governor certified that the ticket favoring Philadelphia had won. The losers petitioned the House, but it eventually supported the men certified by the governor.

The authors of the Constitution had to guess at state populations when they apportioned seats in the first House. As a result the forty-three Congressional districts varied greatly in size. James Jackson, the impassioned orator from Georgia, represented only 16,250 people, while George Thatcher of the Maine district of Massachusetts represented 96,550. Theodore Sedgwick of western Massachusetts had twice as many constituents as his friend Fisher Ames of the Boston district. The population can be estimated almost exactly since the First Congress implemented Article I, Section 2, paragraph 3 of the Constitution early in 1790 by providing for the first census. James Madison's attempt to use the census to gather statistics on occupations was defeated by the Senate. As he complained to Thomas Jefferson, the Senate considered it "as a waste of trouble and supplying materials for idle people to make a book."[2] The first census was taken in 1790 and 1791 and the results used to reapportion the Third Congress.

During the election campaigns and well into 1789, Americans made clear how much they expected from the First Federal Congress. James Iredell, later a Supreme Court Justice, told the North Carolina Ratification Convention in July 1788 that "the first session of Congress will probably be the most important of any for many years. A general code of laws will then be established in execution of every power contained in the Constitution."[3] "No future session of Congress, will ever have so arduous and weighty a charge on their hands," observed the influential *Gazette of the United States*.[4] The task would require "men of the first abilities and of the strictest integrity. . . . Men of less abilities may afterwards answer; but not of less integrity."[5] No one expressed the expectations more succinctly than Samuel Osgood, later Postmaster General, who considered "the first Congress as a second convention."[6]

What made the task particularly challenging was the necessity of interpreting the meaning of the Constitution. Questions about the balance of power between the states and the federal government and among the three branches of the latter still required interpretation. "Among other difficulties," complained Madison, "the exposition of the Constitution is frequently a copious source, and must continue so until its meaning on all great points shall have been settled by precedents."[7] Senator

William Few of Georgia agreed: "we find almost every Act involves great Constitutional principles which requires time and much disquisition to establish."[8]

Congressmen knew that, in addition to these legislative tasks, constituents expected them to provide a variety of services. Many Americans wrote their congressmen seeking federal jobs, and congressmen transmitted their requests and the accompanying letters of political and professional recommendation to the president. The most time consuming constituent service by far, they knew, would be assisting individuals with private claims against the federal government. Many members had constituents who had petitioned the Confederation Congress unsuccessfully and were waiting for the opportunity to appeal to the new Congress. Indeed, the First Federal Congress was inundated with more than six hundred petitions. While many dealt with legislation, the vast majority sought resolution of private claims. Most of these came from Revolutionary War soldiers or their survivors requesting back pay, settlement of accounts, or disability pensions. Other petitioners sought compensation for property confiscated or destroyed during the war, or replacements for federal debt certificates they had lost or stolen. Near the close of the First Congress, Sen. Paine Wingate of New Hampshire reflected that if the host of private petitions which had been submitted "were all to be gratifyed [it] would nearly swallow up the whole revenue."[9]

Members of the First Congress worried about the dangers of these great expectations. Senator Robert Morris of Pennsylvania expressed concern that the

> public expectation seems to be so highly wound up that I think disappointment must inevitably follow after a while, notwithstanding that I believe there will be inclination and abilities in the two houses to do every thing that reasonable and sensible men can promise to themselves, but you know well how impossible it is for public measures to keep pace with the sanguine desires of the interested, the ignorant, and the inconsiderate parts of the Community.[10]

Pennsylvania's other senator, William Maclay, feared that "a prevailing disposition, to treat every thing with great respect, that proceeds from the New Congress will prevent our obtaining that free information, which alone can be Useful to Us at Present."[11]

Senator Paine Wingate of New Hampshire also expressed concern that public expectations would be raised too high. He cautioned Jeremy Belknap to remember that Congress was but a collective body of men subject to many biases and passions and noted local prejudice as the most dangerous of these. Geopolitically aware Americans recognized two major sectional divisions within the United States. That between North and South was easiest to discern because of the prevalence of slavery below the Mason-Dixon Line. Defining the divisions among the South, the Middle States, and the Eastern or New England States was more difficult. New York was sometimes included with the Middle States and sometimes with the Eastern States, but was not considered a New England State. Connecticut, Maryland, and Virginia were sometimes included with the Middle States, and Pennsylvania with the Southern States. There was not and cannot be agreement on precise groupings.

Sectional consciousness, sectional power within the Union, and the threat of dissolution influenced politics throughout the Revolution as much as they would in later years. As the First Congress convened, a Virginia newspaper writer warned that the North had best consider western and southern interests, "or we shall shortly, very shortly perhaps, have another Congress at Richmond."[12] Such public discussion of disunion was not unusual. Less than a year after a Constitution had been ratified by the narrowest of margins, a threat of disunion did not seem so exaggerated to Americans as it does to their descendants. During the First Congress, Americans realized that "southern & northern will often be the division of Congress— The thought is disagreeable; but the distinction is founded in nature, & will last as long as the Union."[13]

The diverse issues and expectations facing the First Federal Congress in 1789 had to be confronted in a political context, the basic complexion of which remained unchanged since the Confederation Congress had struggled with most of the same issues. What had changed, and changed dramatically, was the constitutional context. The Constitution created a central government endowed with powers whose absence had crippled Congress under the Articles of Confederation.

Federal Hall on Wall Street, 1798 watercolor by Archibald Robertson
(Courtesy of the New-York Historical Society).

I

A New Beginning: Congress Convenes in New York

About sunset the Captain of artillery at the fort discharged thirteen guns—bidding farewell to the articles of confederation. This morning just as the sun rose, he fired eleven, emblematical of the eleven States that have adopted the new Constitution. (Portland, Maine, *Cumberland Gazette*, March 19, 1789)

Late in February 1789, the members of the First Federal Congress began to gather in New York, the temporary capital of the fledgling country, a bustling port town of 29,000 persons at the mouth of the Hudson River. By 1789 the city included only the lower tip of Manhattan Island. The number of houses has been estimated at 4,200. On the east side of the island, Byard's Lane (present day Broome Street) was the northern boundary. The west side was settled only as far north as present day Reade Street. Both the Bowery and Greenwich Village were farming areas. During the late 1780's New York was still rebuilding after the great fires of 1776 and 1778 and recovering from the British occupation during much of the Revolutionary War.

The city, hoping to retain its status as the United States capital for as long as possible, made elaborate preparations to welcome the new federal government. As soon as the Confederation Congress resolved the question of where the new government should meet, the City Council charged architect Pierre L'Enfant with the task of creating a comfortable and elegant meeting place in the building that had previously housed the Stamp Act Congress in 1765 and the Confederation Congress from 1785 to 1789. After considerable remodelling at a cost of $65,000, financed by lotteries and a special local tax, the New York City Hall was turned over to Congress for its use.

As reconstructed by L'Enfant, Federal Hall measured 95 feet in width and 145 feet at its deepest point. A plainly appointed hall and four smaller rooms, two of which served as the caretaker's apartment, were situated on the Wall Street side of the first floor off a covered walk on the street. From the hall one entered the central three-story vestibule, which had a marble floor and an ornamented skylight under a cupola. Off this vestibule stood the House of Representatives chamber, a two-story, richly decorated octagonal room. An office for the Clerk of the House and one or more committee rooms were connected to the chamber.

Access to the upper floors was gained by two stairways in the vestibule, one of them reserved for congressmen. The Wall Street side of the second floor consisted of the forty by thirty foot, two-story Senate chamber and several smaller rooms connected to it, including the "machinery room," used to display models of inventions, the Senate secretary's office, and the Senate committee room or rooms. Also on this side was the balcony on which Washington would take the oath of office, located above the covered walk along Wall Street. Two lobbies surrounded the staircases; the one at the head of the public staircase displayed paintings, some by John Trumbull, while the other probably served as an audience area. At the back of the second floor were the two public galleries overhanging the House chamber. Little is known about the third story except that it contained several small rooms, one of which housed the New York Society Library.

Newspaper articles at the time of the building's reopening praised its federal style and reported: "It is solely to the public spiritedness of our Citizens, that we may attribute the erection of such a superb edifice—an edifice that would grace any Metropolis in Europe; . . . by far the most extensive and elegant of any in America."[14] On the other hand, certain individuals suspected the motives of New York's citizens. Representative Frederick A. Muhlenberg of Pennsylvania wrote home, "The Building is really elegant & well designed—for a Trap—but I still hope, however well contrived we shall find Room to get out of it."[15] The building, at Wall and Nassau streets, served as the home for the Congress until the end of its second session in August of 1790. Unfortunately it was allowed to fall into disrepair and was demolished in 1812.

While members of Congress, other than the Pennsylvanians who used every opportunity to laud Philadelphia, agreed that Federal Hall was a fine meeting place, some were not so enthusiastic about city life. Representative Elias Boudinot of New Jersey wrote his wife after a trip home that when he reached "this dirty City—The difference of the wholesome Country Air, from the Stench of the filthy Streets was so apparent, as to effect our smelling Faculties greatly."[16]

New York's residents welcomed the new Congress with elaborate celebrations to symbolize the great hopes that the people of the country had for the new government. On March 4, 1789, the date set for its convening, they marked the occasion with the ringing of church bells, the displaying of flags, and the firing of cannons. "The old government has gently fallen asleep—and the new one is waking into activity," one correspondent, probably Representative George Thatcher, described the peaceful transfer of power in a Maine newspaper. "Let this serve as one instance at least of people that have power laying it down with pleasure, while they see it with great additions passing into the hands of others."[17] Rep. Fisher Ames of Massachusetts, who would become an eloquent spokesman for the Federalists, was more cautious: "The feds have too much faith in its *good*, and the anti's too much forecast of its *ill* tendencies. Both will be baulked probably."[18]

The members who made it to that first day's session found the House and Senate Chambers still under construction, but since both houses lacked the quorum

New-York, March 14.

Yesterday arrived the sloop Delight, Campbell, from Bermuda, and sloop Hancock, Brown, Rhode-Island.

Same day cleared at the Custom-House, sloop Betsey, Gaul, Wilmington.

The exertions of the inhabitants of this City, (says a Correspondent) to accommodate the Grand Congress of the United States, with a building suitable to their dignity, are truly worthy of Record, and entitle them to the grateful acknowledgements of their Fellow-citizens, not only in this State, but in every part of the Union.—Their readiness and liberality in this respect stand unprecedented, and sufficiently evince their patriotic disposition to support the honour and dignity of the national government.—Though the expence of the building will finally be liquidated by a tax on the City and County at large, yet it is solely to the public spiritedness of our Citizens, that we may attribute the erection of such a superb Edifice—an Edifice that would grace any Metropolis in Europe;—and it is to those Gentlemen, who so voluntarily and chearfully lent their credit for this purpose, that we are indebted for the state of perfection to which it has been brought, a state which few could expect at so short a period.

The convenience and elegance of Fœderal Hall, (continues our Correspondent) must afford infinite pleasure to the Honourable Body for whose reception it was erected—For them, it will be pleasing to behold in our Citizens, such a striking instance of their attachment to them, as the immediate Representatives of the People of this extensive Empire, and it is sincerely hoped, will inspire them with a predilection for our Capital, insomuch as to induce them to fix upon it as the place of their permanent residence, for which, beyond all manner of doubt, it is much better calculated than any other City upon the Continent;—and for us it will be a joyful sensation to reflect, that we have not only fulfilled our duty as Members and Brethren of a Community, who have one common interest for their object, but also, that we have tended to the aggrandizement of the Union, and extended our influence as much as possible to promote the respectability of the general government.

Certainly, (says another Correspondent) no building under similar circumstances, was ever erected with such rapidity, and with such taste and judgement of construction, as Fœderal Hall.—This Building, though by far the most extensive and elegant of any in America, has not been six months in raising;—and when it is considered, that since its first commencement, the most difficult and unfavourable season has been to be encountered, surely no one will hesitate to pronounce it a rare enterprize and an astonishing performance;—and it must be acknowledged, that the Commissioners, Architect, and persons employed at it, deserve much praise and commendation.—Let us all hope, that as the Building of this House has been attended with singular success, so may our wishes be fulfilled in every respect;—and long may that distinguished and Honourabe Body, for whose reception and convenience we have thus exerted ourselves, reside among us, and amplify our merits by a wise and successful administration of Government, conveyed by the Trump of Fame from the Dome of Fœderal Hall.

A Commentary on Federal Hall. New York *Morning Post and Daily Advertiser*, March 14, 1789 (Courtesy of Dyer-York Library and Museum, Saco, Maine).

necessary to proceed with business, this was not a real problem. Only thirteen House members showed up, out of fifty-nine expected from the eleven states that had ratified. Eight senators attended. The members of both bodies remained together for less than an hour, and then, disappointed at their inability to begin their momentous work, returned to their lodgings.

Who were the men that composed this Congress that the nation awaited with such hope and expectation? Every member was a white male of Western European ancestry, while white males made up about forty-seven percent of the total population. The law was the primary career stepping stone to political office. Other First Congress members came from the ranks of planters, merchants, ministers, and appointed officeholders. Most of the northern members were professionals or merchants while the South elected primarily planter-landholders, a continuation of the pattern of selecting congressmen from among the ruling interests of the states that had prevailed during the Continental and Confederation Congresses. Only two members of the First Federal Congress had no previous public service before their election to Congress. Generally the election of a member simply continued a career in local, state, or national service. Twenty members of the First Congress had been delegates to the Federal Convention in 1787. Of these, nine served in the House and eleven in the Senate.

At the end of January 1789, George Washington surveyed the names of the men elected to the First Congress and concluded, "on account of the self-created respectability and various talents of its Members, [it] will not be inferior to any Assembly in the world."[19] Correct though he might have been, others had a different view. The practical Madison observed, "I see on the lists of Representatives a very scanty proportion who will share in the drudgery of business."[20] Representative Abraham Baldwin of Georgia even concluded that the choices were not so good in general as those made to the Confederation Congress. Only time would tell if the men described by Representative Fisher Ames as "sober, solid, old-charter folks" could work together successfully on the legislative agenda before them.[21]

Over the ensuing two centuries a two party system, with the accompanying party platforms, loyalties, and structures, has evolved and become a given in any analysis of how Congress accomplishes its business. But students of the Congress of 1789 have no easy labels to classify the members who gathered in New York. The only available litmus test is their position on ratification of the Constitution. Only thirteen of the sixty-six men who would eventually serve in the House and four (three of them from Virginia) of the twenty-nine members of the first Senate were Antifederalists. Although the new Congress was dominated by friends of the Constitution, it must be kept in mind that divisions in the First Federal Congress were based as much upon sectional differences as upon political philosophies, with related economic interests also a factor.

Members of the First Federal Congress left their law practices, businesses, and farms to represent their states in Congress. Only a half dozen or so chose to bring their wives to the seat of government. For the rest this meant a separation from their families for periods as long as eight months while serving their country. They took up residence in New York City's boarding houses and averaged less than one trip home per session. During this enforced separation, those members whose wives enjoyed discussing politics with their friends often sent home detailed letters about congressional affairs.

Two hundred years ago wives and other family members managed the family business or farm, with only letters from New York or Philadelphia as guidance. Meanwhile the absent family head concentrated almost exclusively on the business before the Congress. Members, having no property or other responsibilities in New York, used their spare time for corresponding with their families and constituents, walks in the "countryside" north to Greenwich Village, horseback riding, the theater, informal gatherings at taverns, levees at George Washington's residence, and dinners in the homes of prominent New Yorkers. Boat trips up the Hudson River or to New Jersey and pleasure tours on Manhattan and Long Islands were also popular pastimes. These recreational and social activities provided opportunities for informal discussions and coalition building. They were an important factor in helping members of the First Federal Congress to deal with their important legislative agenda by transcending their political and regional differences.

Speaker of the House Frederick Augustus Muhlenberg of Pennsylvania
by Joseph Wright (Courtesy of the National Portrait Gallery, Smithsonian
Institution).

II

Setting Precedent: Organizing Itself

We are in a wilderness without a single footstep to guide us. It is consequently necessary to explore the way with great labour and caution. Those who may follow will have an easier task. (Rep. James Madison of Virginia to James Madison, Sr., July 5, 1789, *Papers of Madison*, 12:278)

All new governments and administrations set precedents by taking symbolic as well as substantive actions at their inception. Before the new Congress could confront such basic issues as the balance of power between the states and the federal government and the relationships among the three branches of the latter, certain procedural decisions needed to be made. These actions served to set the style of the government and give indications of the direction it would take.

Senators and representatives who were chosen to represent their states in this critically important Congress were acutely aware of the need to demonstrate the viability of the new constitutional system. At the same time most realized that the legislative agenda facing them could not be accomplished overnight. Thus, their actions during the first few months of the session became doubly important.

A problem that had sometimes plagued the Confederation Congress was an inability to make decisions because it lacked a quorum. Consequently, the members of the First Federal Congress on hand in New York for their first meeting on March 4 were anxious to avoid a similar image of impotence. Although the attendance of four more senators and seventeen representatives was necessary to achieve a quorum, those in New York at first evinced optimism. Senator Robert Morris expected a sufficient number in a day or two.

One week later the senators present took their first official action and wrote to their absent colleagues, urging them to come to New York. A follow up letter went to their still missing eight colleagues on March 18. These actions demonstrated the senators' strong belief that the nation's business was too important to be delayed.

House members grew impatient to proceed with business, particularly the establishment of a system for laying duties on imports. One member complained that a "very great Loss of Revenue is running upon us Every Day by means of the

Delay of the Members to attend."[22] While the representatives took no recorded united action, their private correspondence indicates that members individually implored their missing colleagues to hasten to New York.

As March dragged by, those in New York grew more restive and concerned about the image of powerlessness that was being conveyed. Comments from members reveal both anxiety and irritation. "I am inclined to believe that the languor of the old Confederation is transfused into the members of the New Congress," Rep. Ames observed, while Senator Maclay lamented "that Men should pay so little regard to the important appointments that have evolved on them."[23] Many counted the days and worried that it would be impossible to put any revenue system in place before the spring and summer arrival of the dozens of ships already plying the waters of the Atlantic on their way to American ports. Others feared the loss of public confidence and the respect of foreign nations. The words of constituents, such as the governor of Connecticut who warned that "procrastination must create anxiety in the friends to the Constitution," gave validity to these fears.[24]

It should be noted that although the absence of a quorum prevented members in New York from taking any formal action, they were not idle. Members met at the hall and paid visits to each other, discussing the form of the new government, the organization of the judiciary, and the establishment of a system for raising revenue. But the issue of the eventual location of the seat of government was the primary topic of these conversations.

The House of Representatives finally proceeded to business on April 1, a date some members thought inauspicious, being All Fools' day. They immediately began work on internal House business such as the appointment of a Speaker and doorkeepers and the establishment of rules. Since the results of the electoral vote for president had been widely reported, they carefully balanced the choice of individuals from Virginia and Massachusetts by choosing a Pennsylvanian as their Speaker. Frederick Augustus Muhlenberg of Montgomery County, a minister and Federalist politician who had been educated in Germany and was more fluent in German than English, had presided over the Pennsylvania Assembly and the raucous Pennsylvania Ratifying Convention.

With the attendance of the twelfth senator, Virginia's Richard Henry Lee, on April 6, Congress could count the votes for president and vice president. Charles Thomson and Sylvanus Bourn were dispatched to notify George Washington and John Adams of their election. The inauspicious delay was not a forewarning of future impotence, for any potential negative image was quickly counteracted by an impressive and substantial legislative output.

During the early days of April 1789 the two houses were occupied with choosing staff and defining procedures. The House staff consisted of a clerk and two assistants, a chaplain, a sergeant at arms, and a doorkeeper and his assistant, for a grand total of seven. The Senate lacked a sergeant at arms, but otherwise had the same staff.

The House chose John Beckley of Virginia as its first Clerk. A lawyer and a skilled secretary, he had served the Virginia legislature in several capacities. Unfortunately, his meticulousness outweighed his sense of history, and he routinely eliminated office clutter by destroying loose paper records that he believed were no longer valuable. Consequently, most of the official records which would have detailed step by step how that first House of Representatives drafted the legislation on which our federal government is based were destroyed by its own clerk! In 1814, when the British burned the United States Capitol in retaliation for a similar American action in Canada, the records of the early House of Representatives had long since disappeared.

On the Senate side a political struggle took place over the secretaryship. It involved the future of Charles Thomson, the Secretary of Congress, the only office holder to serve Congress continuously from its dynamic birth in 1774 to its anticlimactic demise in 1789. He had made powerful political friends and enemies during those eventful years. At first Thomson's supporters insisted that he should be rewarded with an important post, such as Secretary of State, but eventually he became one of five candidates for Secretary of the Senate. His enemies in New England and the South opposed him, while many friends from the Middle States supported him vociferously. After many ballots, Samuel Allyne Otis, former Speaker of the Massachusetts House of Representatives and a brother of the early Revolutionary hero, James Otis, Jr., became the Senate's choice. Otis continued as Secretary of the Senate for a quarter century, conscientiously preserving nearly every scrap of paper produced by or sent to the Senate.

Thomson was not in New York to witness Otis's triumph because it had been decided even before Congress had a quorum that he was the proper person to inform George Washington of his unanimous election as president. The honor went to him, Thomson told Washington, because of "my having been long in the confidence of the late Congress & charged with the duties of one of the principal civil departments of government."[25] It was an apt symbol, the Secretary of the Old Congress passing the torch to the executive head of the new government. "Charle ridiculously enough has got himself chosen" to be "Express rider of the Union," Otis mocked.[26] Thomson's supporters continued without success their efforts to create a niche for him in the new government. They failed because of the influence of his enemies and the desire, at least symbolically, to separate the new from the old federal government.

New York, when it ratified the Constitution, had proposed an amendment requiring open sessions of both houses of Congress. While neither house passed a rule governing whether the public, and more importantly reporters, would be allowed to attend the debates, the House decided to open its doors except on those rare occasions when a secret meeting had been called, usually for the discussion of military or Indian policy. On the other hand, the Senate, following the precedent of the Old Congress and the Federal Convention, kept its doors closed to everyone, from the common citizen to the President of the United States.

Nothing exists to suggest that any discussion took place over the decision of the

House of Representatives to open its meetings to the public. Given the recent and reluctant admission by the House of Commons in England that, after decades of struggle, the people could attend its debates, it must have seemed natural for the House, the most democratic component of the new government, to open its doors. Sitting in the House gallery on April 9, the first day of public attendance, was the future constitutional commentator James Kent. Years later he described the event:

> all ranks & degrees of men seemed to be actuated by one common impulse, to fill the galleries, as soon as the doors of the House of Representatives were opened for the first time, & to gaze on one of the most interesting fruits of their struggle, a popular Assembly summoned from all parts of the United States. Col. [Alexander] Hamilton remarked to me that . . . such impatient crowds were evidence of the powerful principle of curiosity. . . . I considered it to be a proud & glorious day, the consummation of our wishes; & that I was looking upon an organ of popular will, just beginning to breathe the Breath of Life, & which might in some future age, much more truly than the Roman Senate, be regarded as "the refuge of nations."[27]

Although editors and reporters for several newspapers sat on the House floor taking notes on the speeches, only a few reported the debates with any consistency. Of the newspapers at New York the most extensive coverage appeared in the *Gazette of the United States*. Its editor, John Fenno, came to New York for the purpose of establishing a Federalist organ to support the new government from its inception. In addition, Thomas Lloyd, a shorthand expert who had taken down the speeches at the Pennsylvania and Maryland ratification conventions, moved to New York City in 1789 to publish the debates. Lloyd sold subscriptions to his *Congressional Register* to members of Congress and others seeking a detailed record. His recently transcribed shorthand notes shed additional light on House debates.

Well before Congress moved to Philadelphia, Lloyd had abandoned his ambitious efforts because of financial difficulties and citizens became solely dependent on newspaper accounts. Fenno's relocated newspaper, Andrew Brown's *Federal Gazette* and John Dunlap's *American Daily Advertiser* provided the most complete coverage at the new capital. Newspapers from Maine to Georgia reprinted the debates from one or more of these sources as soon as they received them. Although congressmen often complained that the reporters quoted them inaccurately, they regularly advised constitutents to read the debates in the newspapers and came strongly to the defense of the reporters when Rep. Aedanus Burke of South Carolina attempted to ban them from the House.

The Senate's deliberations remained closed during the First Congress despite two attempts to open its doors. The first, during the first session, was supported only by the two Virginia Antifederalists and their frequent ally William Maclay of Pennsylvania. The other, after Congress moved to Philadelphia for the third session, failed by a vote of 17-9. Thus, the diary kept by Senator Maclay, which records many of the activities and debates on the Senate floor, takes on tremendous importance. Because of it, we actually know more about the intimate, day-to-day workings of the Senate than we do of the more open House of Representatives.

Thomas Lloyd's shorthand notes, May 5–6, 1789
(Courtesy of the Library of Congress).

Senator William Maclay of Pennsylvania by Nick Ruggieri (Courtesy of Kim Baer, Pennsylvania Bar Association).

Under the Constitution each house of the Congress is required to keep a journal of its proceedings. Samuel Otis sat in the chamber and took rough notes. We know from Maclay's diary that the Secretary read the minutes the next day and the senators attempted to correct them. Maclay, a supporter of Thomson, was extremely critical of Otis's work: "our Secretary makes a most miserable hand of it, the grossest Mistakes made on our minutes and it cost Us an hour or Two to rectify them."[28] After correction, the minutes were copied over by a clerk, checked, and sent to the printer. In the case of the Senate, the journal of proceedings, as printed in the newspapers of the day, provided the only available public record of that body's actions.

The House often made use of the committee of the whole, a parliamentary device by which some member other than the Speaker assumed the chair and the members engaged in debate under less formal rules than in the House. This method of consideration provided an easier opportunity for members to be heard and gave them two chances to amend bills. Rep. Fisher Ames criticized the method as slowing progress: "Our great committee is too unwieldy for this operation. A great, clumsy machine is applied to the slightest and most delicate operations—the hoof of an elephant to the strokes of mezzotinto."[29] The Senate chose to consider most legislation without going into a committee of the whole, but would often spend several days on a "second reading" during which most of the debate and attempts at amendment occurred.

The early months of the first session saw several actions centered around questions of protocol which worked to negate any concept—usually held by senators—that the two Houses of Congress were really an "upper" and a "lower" house. In addition to setting their own rules, the two Houses dealt with such matters as how they would exchange messages, how communications would be sent to and from the executive, and how legislative disagreements would be settled. Certain procedural disputes occurred that resulted in a leveling out of the prestige and image of the two houses. One such conflict arose over the method for delivering messages between the two houses.

The original joint committee report on these communications, accepted by the Senate and sent to the House, proposed that bills or other messages from the Senate would be delivered by its Secretary, while the House would send two members to deliver a bill to the Senate and one member to deliver other messages. Maclay reports that the House's reaction to this assertion of superiority on the part of the Senate was laughter. After lengthy consideration and reconsideration, the Senate was forced to accept messages delivered to it by the Clerk of the House.

Later in the session, Congress made another decision that contradicted the theory of Senate superiority. The Senate majority tried to ensure that there would be a discrimination in the daily pay of representatives and senators, with senators being paid more. Although James Madison supported this concept in the House, he lacked the votes to gain approval. The bill passed by the House provided for a daily pay of six dollars for both senators and representatives.

The Senate responded by resolving that there ought to be a discrimination between the salaries and amended the bill to provide for an increase to seven dollars daily for senators only in 1795. The House's refusal to agree and the Senate's insistence forced a conference on the issue. This committee's report demonstrates how firmly each house held its stance:

> That they had come to no precise agreement—that the Senate could not be induced to recede from their amendment—but by way of compromise, the committee on the part of the Senate proposed, that the compensation provided for by the present bill should be limited to seven years—the last of which the compensation of the Senate to be at 7 dollars—Or, they proposed that the House should pass a law providing for their own compensation, without including the Senate.[30]

The first compromise suggested in the report was accepted. Thus, the Senate may have won a skirmish in the battle to exert a degree of superiority, but the House won the war. For the year 1795, the senators were paid more, but in 1796 the daily compensations were again made equal. This precedent was not broken until fiscal year 1983. For that one year House members actually received higher salaries than senators, while senators were allowed unlimited outside income.

THE Committees of both Houses of Congress, appointed to take order for conducting the ceremonial of the formal reception, &c. of the President of the United States, on Thursday next, have agreed to the following order thereon, viz.

That General Webb, Colonel Smith, Lieutenant-Colonel Fish, Lieut. Col. Franks, Major L'Enfant, Major Bleecker, and Mr. John R. Livingston, be requested to serve as Assistants on the occasion.

That a chair be placed in the Senate-Chamber for the President of the United States. That a chair be placed in the Senate-Chamber for the Vice-President, to the right of the President's chair; and that the Senators take their seats on that side of the chamber on which the Vice-President's chair shall be placed. That a chair be placed in the Senate-Chamber for the Speaker of the House of Representatives, to the left of the President's chair—and that the Representatives take their seats on that side of the chamber on which the Speaker's chair shall be placed.

That seats be provided in the Senate-Chamber sufficient to accommodate the late President of Congress, the Governor of the Western territory, the five persons being the heads of the three great departments, the Minister Plenipotentiary of France, the Encargado de negocios of Spain, the Chaplains of Congress, the persons in the suite of the President; and also to accommodate the following Public Officers of the State, viz. The Governor, the Lieutenant-Governor, the Chancellor, the Chief Justice, and other Judges of the Supreme Court, and the Mayor of the city. That one of the Assistants wait on these gentlemen, and inform them that seats are provided for their accommodation, and also to signify to them that no precedence of seats is intended, and that no salutation is expected from them on their entrance into, or their departure from the Senate-Chamber.

That the members of both Houses assemble in their respective Chambers precisely at twelve o'clock, and that the Representatives preceded by the Speaker, and attended by their Clerk, and other Officers, proceed to the Senate-Chamber, there to be received by the Vice-President and Senators rising.

That the Committees attend the President from his residence to the Senate-Chamber, and that he be there received by the Vice-President, the Senators and Representatives rising, and be by the Vice-President conducted to his chair.

That after the President shall be seated in his Chair, and the Vice-President, Senators and Representatives shall be again seated, the Vice-President shall announce to the President, that the members of both Houses will attend him to be present at his taking the Oath of Office required by the Constitution. To the end that the Oath of Office may be administered to the President in the most public manner, and that the greatest number of the people of the United States, and without distinction, may be witnesses to the solemnity, that therefore the Oath be administered in the outer Gallery adjoining to the Senate Chamber.

That when the President shall proceed to the gallery to take the Oath, he be attended by the Vice-President, and be followed by the Chancellor of the State, and pass through the middle door, that the Senators pass through the door on the right, and the Representatives, preceded by the Speaker, pass through the door on the left, and such of the persons who shall have been admitted into the Senate-Chamber, and may be desirous to go into the gallery, are then also to pass through the door on the right. That when the President shall have taken the Oath, and returned into the Senate-Chamber, attended by the Vice-President, and shall be seated in his chair, that the Senators and the Representatives also return into the Senate-Chamber, and that the Vice-President and they resume their respective seats.

Both Houses having resolved to accompany the President after he shall have taken the Oath, to St. Paul's Chapel, to hear divine service, to be performed by the Chaplain of Congress, that the following order of procession be observed, viz. The door-keeper and messenger of the House of Representatives. The Clerk of the House. The Representatives. The Speaker. The President, with the Vice-President at his left hand. The Senators. The Secretary of the Senate. The door-keeper, and messenger of the Senate.

That a Pew be reserved for the President—Vice-President—Speaker of the House of Representatives, and the Committees; and that pews be also reserved sufficient for the reception of the Senators and Representatives.

That after divine service shall be performed, the President be received at the door of the Church, by the Committees, and by them attended in carriages to his residence.

That it be intrusted to the Assistants to take proper precautions for keeping the avenues to the Hall open, and that for that purpose, they wait on his Excellency the Governor of this State, and in the name of the Committees request his aid, by an order or recommendation to the Civil Officers, or militia of the city, to attend and serve on the occasion, as he shall judge most proper.

April 29th, 1789.

Joint committee report on the Ceremonial for the Inauguration of the President, April 29, 1789 (Courtesy of the Library of Congress).

III

An Imperial Presidency?

Our new Government is now in full Operation, but how it will move or what will be the End of it I can scarcely conjecture. I am not yet in Love with it, & I doubt if I ever shall be. With Concern I perceive that it has infused into the Minds of People here the most intolerable Rage for Monarchy that can be imagined. Verily I believe that a very great Proportion are ripe for a King & would salute the President as such with all the Folly of Enthusiasm. . . . This Spirit has been prevailing here for a great while, but I was in hopes that when they saw that the Senators were but Men & even the President but a Man, the Rage would subside. This however is not the Case & nothing is talked of but Titles for the President & Vice President. If this Folly was not encouraged it might in Time wear off. But unfortunately the Wisdom of the Senate gives it Sanction. (Rep. Thomas Tudor Tucker of South Carolina to St. George Tucker, May 13, 1789, Tucker-Coleman Papers, Swem Library, College of William and Mary)

The forces at the Federal Convention that pressed for a strong federal government saw a powerful executive as an essential ingredient. When the delegates created the presidency, they knew the position would be filled by the man who presided over their deliberations: the American hero, former Commander in Chief of the Continental Army, George Washington. They knew that only he could unite Americans behind the new government, giving Congress the time needed to deal with its pressing agenda and to confront the many potentially divisive issues before it. As the symbol of American independence and virtue, he commanded enormous respect from the American people. Indeed, his presidency of the Federal Convention and support for the Constitution probably had made the crucial difference in 1787 and 1788.

The responsibility for implementing the institution of the presidency rested with Congress. One of its first tasks was to count the votes cast by the electors in the states and declare the election of George Washington as president and John Adams as vice president. Each elector had two votes. Washington was elected unanimously, but Adams received only thirty-four of a possible sixty-nine. His closest rival, John Jay, received nine votes. Recognizing the danger of a tie vote, Alexander Hamilton had worked to prevent it. In the New York legislature, Federalists and Antifederalists could not agree on a method for choosing electors, and so New York did not participate in the first presidential election. Hamilton shifted his activities to Connecticut, where he saw to it that the electors split their votes among three, rather than two, individuals. His efforts proved unnecessary because several of the electors, especially in Maryland and South Carolina, voted for favorite son candidates.

Despite Washington's professed reluctance to assume the presidency, he sent his acceptance to the president *pro tempore* of the Senate, John Langdon of New Hampshire, on the day that Charles Thomson arrived at Mount Vernon with the official news of his election. Two days later, on April 16, he set out for New York by carriage, accompanied by Thomson and Colonel David Humphreys.

All along the route of his triumphal eight day journey citizens greeted and honored the nation's hero. The celebration was particularly impressive at Philadelphia, where Washington mounted a white horse for the final part of the journey into the city, and he and his party were met and accompanied by mounted troops from Chester and Philadelphia. At Gray's Ferry the citizens had decorated the bridge to create a triumphal arch, and after Washington crossed the bridge, a wreath was placed on his head by a small child. Washington and the troops paraded through crowds of cheering Philadelphians on Market and Second streets. A dinner for two hundred and fifty was held at City Tavern. That evening the celebration continued with a display of fireworks. In order to avoid any appearance of partiality, Washington turned down the invitation of Sen. Robert Morris to stay the night at his home and instead slept at City Tavern.

A number of Philadelphia groups sent congratulatory addresses to Washington. This address of the President and Faculty of the University of Pennsylvania exemplifies them and the many others delivered along the route:

> It is by this honor, (the highest that America can bestow) that a grateful People express the affection which your eminent services have kindled in their bosoms. It is this that has given them but *one voice* in the delegation of this important trust, that unites the homage of the heart with the duty of the Citizen. To be the first Magistrate of a great Empire, is a situation that many have attained: but to acquire it by the *unanimous* voice of a *free* people, is an event as rare in the history of the world as those illustrious virtues of which it is the just reward.[31]

On April 23 George Washington arrived in New York by boat, escorted by a committee of senators and representatives who had gone to the New Jersey shore as an official escort. As the specially constructed barge crossed the Hudson River, many ships and small boats in the harbor displayed their colors and naval ornaments while porpoises leapt about the barge. As the president elect approached the New York shore, a Spanish ship hoisted onto its rigging the flags of two dozen nations and sounded a thirteen gun salute as the crew manned its yards. A grand celebration heralded Washington's entrance into the city with a thirteen cannon salute, military units, red carpets, strains of "God Save the King," and an adoring crowd of several thousand who lined the shore for a half mile from the Battery to the Paulus Hook Ferry landing.

Antifederalist Governor George Clinton welcomed Washington in a ceremony and at a dinner that evening, publicly acknowledging that the executive head of the federal government took precedence over the executive head of a state government. Citizens lined the streets as a procession moved through the city from the Hudson to the presidential mansion on Cherry Street near the East River. Elegantly appointed by the cultured taste of two of the city's most prominent ladies, the redecorated house was wallpapered on two floors, carpeted with the best Turkish rugs, and seemingly filled with silver and fine china. New York marked the occasion that evening with fireworks and illuminations. The outpouring of feeling at these jubilant demonstrations caused some uneasiness among members of Congress, who feared the adulation could convert the president into an elected monarch.

Someone who disapproved of this virtual deification of Washington—probably an enemy he had made in his political and military career—satirized the spirit of the occasion. On the day after his election, two weeks before his triumphal entrance into New York City, a cartoon entitled "The Entry" was hawked on the streets of the capital. In it, Washington rode a jackass, led by his aide David Humphreys who chanted hosannahs. A couplet stated:

> The glorious time has come to pass
> When David shall conduct an Ass.[32]

Although the cartoon must have shocked New Yorkers almost as much as it did those who in the succeeding two centuries have apparently destroyed all copies of it, its powerful message reminds us that even George Washington was not above the criticism of his contemporaries.

A joint committee of Congress planned a respectful yet simple ceremony for administering the oath of office to Washington. On the day designated for the inauguration, April 30, the new president chose to wear a brown suit of American-made cloth and a symbolic sword, rather than his military uniform. This struck just the note that the majority in Congress was anxious to have heard. The leader of the new government should be held in high esteem but not worshipped. He would be a strong leader, chosen from among the people. Despite Congress's efforts, a young witness later reflected that the ceremony had been a coronation.

After the public swearing-in on the balcony of Federal Hall, the Congress and the President retired to the Senate chamber for the inaugural address. Senator Maclay of Pennsylvania described the scene:

> this great Man was agitated and embarrassed more than ever he was by the levelled Cannon or pointed Musket. he trembled, and several times could scarce make out to read, tho it must be supposed he had often read it before. . . . When he came to the Words all the World, he made a flourish with his right hand, which left rather an ungainly impression.[33]

Washington's short address focused on his commitment to and hopes for the new system of government established by "the important revolution just accomplished."[34] Other than recommending that Congress consider the question of amendments to the Constitution, which had been widely raised during ratification and the first federal election, he made only one substantive proposal. He asked that he receive only his expenses rather than a salary, a proposal later rejected by the Congress. Washington had originally considered a much longer inaugural address which asserted a philosophy of presidential leadership by making recommendations on a variety of legislative matters. It had been drafted for him by David Humphreys, an advocate of a president as much like a monarch as was politically feasible in the United States. In December 1788, en route home for his difficult congressional campaign, Madison spent a week with Washington at Mount Vernon, engaged in detailed discussions about the new government. Soon thereafter, Washington sent Madison a copy of the proposed address. Madison considered it politically disastrous and advised strongly against its use, a course of action which the president elect adopted. Forty years later the first editor of Washington's papers, Jared Sparks, asked Madison to identify seventy-three mysterious folio pages written in Washington's fine, clear hand. Sparks took Madison's expression of regret that the document had survived as permission to cut it into snippets for souvenir hunters. Its remnants convey the haughty tone of a superior lecturing important inferiors.

On April 22 the Senate began consideration of an issue which would occupy it intermittently for the next three weeks: the question of titles of address for the president and vice president. The subject was raised by Richard Henry Lee of Virginia, who moved for a joint committee. Maclay believed the "base business" had been taken up only because of Vice President John Adams's interest in it.[35] Indeed, Adams, who assumed an activist role as presiding officer of the Senate, pursued the subject avidly. He believed the Federal Convention had created too weak an executive branch. Proper titles would enhance the elective presidency, command the respect of the people and of foreign nations, and lead to a more politically stable society. Maclay, believing the matter too absurd to merit consideration, failed to stop the appointment of the committee.

Although the Senate appointees were three political allies of the vice president, the report of the joint committee stated simply that no titles should be used other than President and Vice President of the United States. The House quickly agreed to the report, but the Senate rejected it after a lengthy debate in which Lee and Maclay were the chief protagonists. While Maclay's views represented those of the Senate minority, House members stood virtually unanimous in their opposition to titles. With images of red carpets and the memories of "God Save the King" fresh in their minds, a majority in Congress did not wish to endow the office of the presidency, or even its special first occupant, with monarchical trappings.

For several days the Senate's time was consumed by extensive and repetitive debate on this issue. A special Senate committee on titles was appointed to recon-

From A decent respect for the opinion and practise of civilized Nations, whether under Monarchical or Republican forms of government, whose custom is to annex titles of respectability to the office of their Chief Magistrate; and that on intercourse with foreign nations a due respect for the Majesty of the people of the United States may not be hazarded by an ~~affectation~~ *appearance* of singularity; ~~have induced~~ *have been induced* the Senate *^* to be of opinion that it would be proper to annex *a* respectable Title to the office of President of the United States;

But the Senate desirous of preserving harmony with the House of Representatives, who the practice lately observed in presenting an Address to the President was without the addition of Title, think it proper for the present to act in conformity with the practice of that ~~other~~ House Therefore resolved that the present Address be 'to the President of the United States; without addition of Title,

~~Accepted.~~

Senate resolution on a title for the President, May 14, 1789
(Courtesy of the National Archives).

sider the issue and confer with a House committee on the disagreement existing between the two houses. On May 14 it reported failure to agree with the House and the opinion that the president should be addressed as "His Highness the President of the United States of America, and Protector of their Liberties." In a strongly worded resolution stating its continued belief in the need for a respectable title for the office of president, the Senate capitulated for the sake of preserving harmony with the House and agreed "that the present address be—'To the President of the United States'"—without addition of title.[36]

Although the debate on titles had ended in both houses, John Adams continued to express his opinion that titles were essential. He feared:

> the Contempt, the Scorn and the Derision of all Europe, while you call your national Conductor, General or President. You may depend on another Thing. The State Government will ever be uppermost in America in the Minds of our own People, till you give a superiour Title to your first national Magistrate.[37]

Unfortunately for Adams, one of the most powerful advocates of the cause of American independence, his outspoken support of titles and other monarchical embellishments led some members of the First Federal Congress to lose respect for him and to ridicule his position. From the House galleries Maclay witnessed representatives passing notes back and forth. The following clever riddle by Thomas Tudor Tucker of South Carolina and John Page of Virginia may have been among them:

> Quis ? by T.T.T.M.D.
> In gravity clad,
> He has nought in his Head,
>   But Visions of Nobles & Kings,
> With Commons below,
>   Who respectfully bow,
>   And worship the dignified *Things*
>
>   The Answer Impromtu' by P
> I'll tell in a Trice—
>   'Tis Old Daddy *Vice*
> Who carries of Pride an Ass-load;
>   Who turns up his Nose,
>   Wherever he goes
> With Vanity swell'd like a Toad[38]

The decision on titles stands as a real and symbolic last step on the road towards breaking with monarchical traditions, a process begun in 1776. The celebrations in honor of Washington remained simply a testimony to the people's love for their national hero, and were not translated into the forms or power of an imperial presidency. The conclusion of the titles debate was another victory for the House and for democratic institutions.

IV

The First Federal Revenues

The House of Representatives entered upon that Subject immediately after they formed. and have agreed upon the rates of the impost on the various articles; in doing which they had respect to revenue, and the encouraging the manufactures of these States, much time was necessarily taken up in adjusting those rates to Suit the circumstances of the different parts of the union, a spirit of harmony & accommodation has been manifested. (Rep. Roger Sherman of Connecticut to Oliver Wolcott, May 14, 1789, Wolcott Papers, Connecticut Historical Society)

The establishment of revenue sources for the federal government was one of the most important tasks the First Federal Congress faced. Without a source of income, public credit could not be established, the costs of government could not be met, and the interest on the huge Revolutionary War debt could not be paid.

The failure of the Confederation Congress to establish for itself a revenue independent of the states had been a major limitation on its ability to function adequately. In 1781 Congress asked the states to amend the Articles of Confederation so that it could place a five percent tariff on imported goods. Amendment of the Articles required unanimity and Rhode Island rejected the Amendment. Congress tried again in 1783, this time placing specific duties on wines, liquors, teas, molasses, and a few other similar items, while assessing the five percent on all other imported goods. Again one state, this time New York, refused to ratify. Nevertheless, the attempt proved useful to the First Congress, for it worked from a modified version of the 1783 Amendment when it drew up the first federal revenue act.

According to the Constitution, all revenue bills must originate in the House. The representatives recognized that the issue took precedence over such other important matters as the creation of the executive departments and Amendments to the Constitution. James Madison took the lead in the debate, which opened two days after the House formed a quorum. A decision was quickly made in favor of taking the time to devise a permanent rather than a temporary system, even if that meant losing revenues on goods imported into the United States during the spring of 1789. Senator William Maclay and others were convinced that the delay continued because influential merchants, some of them members of Congress, sought to avoid the new

View of New York Harbor from Brooklyn by John Montresor
(Courtesy of the Library of Congress).

duties as long as possible. A fellow merchant from Philadelphia, considering the
double capacity in which Rep. Thomas Fitzsimons acted, concluded *"You will always
find the Merchant Uppermost."*[39]

By August Congress had passed the four bills which formed the basis of the
federal revenue system. The impost (or tariff, as we have come to call it) and tonnage
bills raised the revenues, while the collection and coasting bills provided for
enforcement.

The impost bill levied a five percent tariff on all goods imported except for an
extensive list of goods on which specific duties were enumerated. A select committee
presented the impost bill on 5 May. The House debated the bill for almost two weeks
before sending it to the Senate. The length of time devoted to the bill reflected both
political and procedural problems.

The procedural problems arose because the bill was the first major one considered by the House and its methods for doing business had not been tested. The
major political dispute arose between New Englanders and Southerners over how
much of a tariff should be levied on molasses, imported primarily by New England.
New England argued that a tax on the commodity would be unpopular just as it had
been when levied by the British. Madison replied:

> if this is to be adduced as a proof of the popularity of a measure, what are we to say
> with respect to a tax on tea? Gentlemen remembered, no doubt, how odious this
> kind of tax was thought to be throughout America, yet the house had, without
> hesitation, laid a considerable duty upon it. He did not imagine that a duty on either
> of those articles were in themselves objectionable, it was the principle upon which
> the tax was laid, that made them unpopular under the British government.[40]

In the end, the House resolved even the dispute over the molasses tax with little more than rhetorical pleas on the floor. According to Rep. Thomas Fitzsimons, these were delivered in large part to satisfy constituents. Indeed, many members expressed surprise at how little sectional rancor arose, considering the different economies of the Eastern, Middle, and Southern States and the relationship of those economies to the tariffs proposed on specific items. Madison went so far as to tell the House that Virginia would not have been so hesitant to ratify the Constitution had it known how smoothly the North and South would reach consensus on the first federal revenue bill.

At least one member concluded that the desire to avoid direct taxes on individuals and an excise on domestic distilled liquor had led the House to impose import duties which he considered too high. Representatives also divided over the issue of how much the duties should be used to encourage American manufacturing. Even before Congress achieved a quorum, constituents petitioned for protective duties on certain items. By the time the First Congress adjourned in 1791, it had heard from individuals and groups in support of duties on glass, cotton goods, coaches, mustard, rope, hemp, tobacco products, and liquor.

In 1790 Congress replaced the impost act with a ways and means act to raise the additional revenues required by the funding of the national debt. And, in need of a new source of revenue to pay for the assumption of the state Revolutionary War debts by the federal government, Congress agreed in 1791 to the duties on distilled spirits or excise act.

The second revenue bill considered by the First Congress was the tonnage bill, which provided that each vessel entering a port in the United States must pay a duty based on its carrying capacity in tons. Its cornerstone was a discrimination among American built and owned ships, American built but foreign owned ships, and all other ships. The Confederation Congress had long sought such discriminatory power, which, however, was not authorized by the Articles of Confederation. Now, under the Constitution, Congress could differentiate between American and foreign shipping, and some towns eagerly petitioned for this kind of legislation.

The assessment on "all other ships"—the foreign owned and built—caused a controversy. Madison proposed, and the House accepted, a discrimination in the duty paid by foreign owned vessels: thirty cents on ships owned by citizens of nations with whom the United States had a commercial treaty and fifty cents on the ships of other nations. The goal of the members supporting the amendment was to distinguish between Great Britain and those friendly nations with whom the United States had commercial treaties, especially France. They argued that the necessity for discrimination as a means of encouraging American shipping had been one of the reasons for the political revolution which had given the United States its new Constitution. The Senate deleted this added discrimination from the bill, arguing in part that something of a more serious nature was necessary to counter British restrictions on American trade. When the House stood firm, the first conference committee in congressional history made an unsuccessful attempt to resolve the

Representative John Laurance of New York City by John Trumbull (Courtesy of the New-York Historical Society). Laurance, a lawyer and Federalist, was the most active member of the state's delegation in the House of Representatives.

difference. In order to save the bill, the House then accepted the Senate amendment. An attempt to establish a similar discrimination died in the House in 1790.

Could the federal government collect the duties it had levied on a society whose extensive coast line and anti-British politics had turned the practice of smuggling goods past British revenue agents into an art? One of the longest and most detailed acts adopted by the First Congress, the Collection Act of July 1789, assured that federal revenues would not be evaded by establishing collection districts, each with a port of entry at which resided new federal officials, a collector, naval officer, and surveyor. Other ports in the district were designated as ports of delivery only, and all ships bound for them had to stop first at the port of entry to declare its cargo and pay the federal duties. The revenue officials had powers of search and seizure and the act established penalties for violation of federal revenue laws. Rep. John Laurance of New York City was the bill's principal author.

Local political pressure on the members of Congress, as well as geography, influenced which ports were named for entry. For example, Virginia Senator Richard Henry Lee was convinced that his colleague William Grayson had decided privately with Madison how the Potomac River ports would be designated. One of the most significant questions to arise during the debate over the collection act was seen as a major test of the meaning and impact of federalism. Should each state have its own collection district, or could parts of different states be combined into one district when geographical realities argued in favor of such a consolidation? Senator Maclay reported that Congress received "Clouds of Letters" in protest.[41] It then defeated the attempt to combine the Delmarva Peninsula of Maryland, Delaware, and Virginia into one district. In the excise act of 1791 a similar issue arose, and again Congress refused to combine portions of states into federal districts.

The Collection Act called for the appointment of more than one hundred federal officials and can be considered the foundation for both the federal bureaucracy and the federal patronage system. Its revision in 1790 established the United States Coast Guard by authorizing the construction and manning of ten federal revenue cutters, and redesignated some ports of entry and delivery in response to petitions from constituents.

The fourth revenue related act of the first session made further regulations to see that revenue laws were not evaded. The coasting act established federal forms for registering and clearing all vessels plying American coastal waters and regulated the domestic, undutied trade among the states up and down the Atlantic Coast. The forms it required created a new category of federal record.

In 1790 Congress passed special acts to extend the provisions of its four basic revenue laws to North Carolina and Rhode Island after they ratified the Constitution. Before that, in response to petitions from these states, Congress had treated them as if they were part of the union. Other less important acts supplemented the federal revenue and regulatory system.

Despite complaints, especially from South Carolina Federalists and Antifederalists, that the bill was an infringement on the rights of the states, under the lighthouses act of August 1789 the United States assumed the cost of the maintenance of all lighthouses, beacons, and buoys which had previously been erected by the states to render navigation safe and easy. The act also called on the states to cede ownership and jurisdiction over all such facilities to the United States within one year or reassume their costs. Later revisions of the act gave the states until 1792 to cede the property to the United States before losing federal funding. The 1789 act also provided for the erection of a lighthouse at the mouth of Chesapeake Bay at federal expense. A year later Congress agreed to complete the lighthouse which Massachusetts had begun at Portland Head in the district of Maine. Thus did the First Congress assert the Constitution's grant of control over coastal navigational facilities to the federal government.

In 1790 an inspection act made certain that federal officials saw to it that goods subject to inspection by state law were so inspected. The merchant seamen act of July 1790 provided federal regulations to govern contracts between American merchant seamen and masters of American vessels. The act also regulated working conditions on shipboard. A bill to regulate harbors and to establish federal hospitals

Congrefs of the United States,

BEGUN and held at the City of NEW-YORK, On Wednefday the fourth of March, one thoufand feven hundred and eighty-nine.

An ACT *making* Appropriations *for the fervice of the* prefent Year.

SEC. I. **B**E it enacted by the Senate and Houfe of Reprefentatives of the *UnitedStates of America in Congrefs affembled,* That there be appropriated for the fervice of the prefent year, to be paid out of the monies which arife, either from the requifitions heretofore made upon the feveral ftates, or from the duties on impoft and tonnage, the following fums, viz. A fum not exceeding two hundred and fixteen thoufand dollars for defraying the expences of the civil lift, under the late and prefent government; a fum not exceeding one hundred and thirty-feven thoufand dollars for defraying the expences of the department of war; a fum not exceeding one hundred and ninety thoufand dollars for difcharging the warrants iffued by the late board of treafury, and remaining unfatisfied; and a fum not exceeding ninety-fix thoufand dollars for paying ﬅe penfions to invalids.

FREDERICK AUGUSTUS MUHLENBERG,
Speaker of the Houfe of Reprefentatives.
JOHN ADAMS, *Vice-Prefident of the United States, and Prefident of the Senate.*
APPROVED September the 29th, 1789.
GEORGE WASHINGTON, *Prefident of the United States.*

Appropriations Act [HR-32], September 29, 1789 (Courtesy of the Clements Library). This act, passed to fund the budget for 1789, is the shortest of its kind in American history.

for the care of sick and disabled American seamen, to be funded by a wage deduction plan, which was proposed during the first session, did not pass until later in the 1790s. A third session bill which attempted to establish to what extent shipowners were liable for damages to the property being transported on their ships also failed to pass. Congress received petitions seeking mitigation of fines and forfeitures arising under the collection and coasting acts. In response, it established an appeal procedure using federal district courts, but granting the final decision to the secretary of the treasury.

In order to appropriate its new revenues to the needs of the federal government, the First Congress adopted three budgets and a special appropriations act. The 1789 budget called for spending $639,000 to cover the costs of running the government, paying invalid pensions, and discharging expenditures authorized by the board of treasury under the Confederation Congress. The 1790 budget was more extensive. It appropriated $541,395.70 to pay federal salaries, the expenses of the department of war, invalid pensions, maintenance of lighthouses, and for several other specified purposes. In addition the act granted the president a $10,000 contingency fund, covered payment of any expenses Congress incurred, and authorized the secretary of the treasury to borrow the money he needed to obtain the sums appropriated in the act. At the end of the second session, in August 1790, Congress adopted a special appropriations act authorizing an additional $233,219.97 for a variety of specific purposes recommended primarily by the secretary of the treasury. The budget for 1791 totaled $740,728.60. All together, the First Federal Congress spent $2,154,344.20 for the first three years of the government's operations.

Each of these budgets was based on reports from the treasury department which listed how every penny appropriated by Congress was to be spent; for example, $354.82 for the annual educational expenses of George M. White Eyes, $121.37 for renovation of offices for the treasury department, and $255.73 for an Indian interpreter. The preciseness of the figures on which the appropriations acts were based illustrate the fiscal control that the federal government had over its budget two hundred years ago.

Richmond Hill Mansion, New York City (Courtesy of the Library of Congress).
The residence of Vice President John Adams and his family, Richmond Hill
mansion was one of New York's most impressive structures. Built in 1767, it was
situated on the road to Greenwich Village, at present day Varick and
Charlton streets.

V

Shaping
the Executive Branch

The House of Representatives have resolved to submit the principal Direction of the finances to a single man. Thro this Measure I can feel the Pulse of our Government. It is vigorous beyond my Hopes, far beyond my Expectations, and comes up to my Wishes. It is the Vigor of Administration which can alone consolidate recent Establishments. . . . The Extent of our Country and the deliberative freedom of its legislative Authority require the Compensation of an active and vigorous Execution. Every subordinate Power should be tied to the Chief by those intermediate Links of Will and Pleasure which like the Elasticity of the arterial System render sensible the Pulsations of the Heart at the remotest Extremities. (Gouverneur Morris to William Carmichael, July 4, 1789, Gouverneur Morris Papers, Library of Congress)

Discussion of the divisive issue of an executive branch of government dated back to 1776. During the Revolutionary War, commitment to government by legislatures and the popular resentment against the king, royal governors, and their ministers proved so powerful that Congress performed executive functions by appointing committees or by delegating them to one of its members. In 1781, in response to a change in its political makeup, Congress created three semi-independent executive departments—war, foreign affairs, and finance—headed by non-delegates. This system continued in effect with only one change until the First Federal Congress acted. The one change took place in 1784, when Congress abolished the powerful office of superintendent of finance and replaced it with a three man board of treasury. Washington appointed Henry Knox, secretary of war since early 1785, to the same office in 1789, and relied on John Jay, secretary for foreign affairs since late 1784, for advice until Secretary of State Thomas Jefferson reached New York City in March 1790.

The framers of the Constitution left the job of fleshing out the executive branch to Congress, thus reaffirming the principle of legislative supremacy. In fact, the duties of the executive departments and the power to create them are in the document only by implication. During its first session Congress passed three "organic" acts relating to the executive branch, laws creating the departments of state (at first known as foreign affairs), treasury, and war. These acts expanded Article II of the Constitution and consequently were constitutional in character, yet subject to repeal by any Congress united enough to overcome a presidential veto.

Some support existed for a fourth department. Friends of Charles Thomson, secretary of the Confederation Congress, hoped he might become head of a home or domestic department. They argued that the federal government should encourage geography, science, technology, navigation, and internal improvements, and that the responsibilities for these and other national functions such as the census, Indian relations, federal records, copyrights, and patents belonged in a separate department. But the majority rejected the home department. Later in the first session, Congress changed the name of the Department of Foreign Affairs to the Department of State and expanded its authority to include many of these domestic functions.

The issuance of copyrights and patents was one of the functions Congress assigned to the state department. Before that, Americans seeking protection for their writings and inventions had no alternative but to petition Congress for a private bill. Authors used this method to request copyrights for books about arithmetic, religious sects, and American history and geography. Inventors asked for patents, and in some cases federal patronage, for inventions to counteract counterfeiters, to improve bridge construction, to determine longitude, to harness steam for energy, to thresh and reap crops, to distill spirits, and to move boats by wheels rather than oars.

Once the revenue system was on its way to enactment, the House of Representatives seized the initiative on the issue of the executive departments. No sooner had Elias Boudinot of New Jersey proposed their creation than James Madison raised a question that precipitated one of the most notable constitutional debates of congressional history. Madison offered a resolution proposing that Congress grant the president explicit power to remove heads of departments. The resolution forced Congress to confront and define basic tenets of constitutional interpretation relating to the meaning of separation of powers, advice and consent, checks and balances, and impeachment.

The questions at issue—who has the power to remove executive officers and how would they do so—arose because, with the exception of impeachment, the Constitution is silent on the issue of removal. It left Congress to decide where the authority rested. During the debate individual members introduced four distinct theories on the removal power. Supporters of each of these viewpoints believed their interpretation was the original intent of the authors of the Constitution.

Representative William L. Smith of South Carolina argued that the only method of removal should be that provided for in the Constitution—impeachment. He adopted the very strict interpretation of the Constitution that executive officers could not be removed unless they were found guilty of some crime or misdemeanor. Smith defended this theory in a letter to a friend who disagreed with his interpretation:

my desire to guard the Constitution from the dangers of legislative constructions, (which may hereafter be productive of considerable injury to our State, whose representation in point of numbers is weak & unequal to that of any other part of the Union) animated me with a peculiar warmth of opposition. There are men of ingenuity in our house, whose tendency to establish a monarchical govt. & whose abilities to promote it would go [to] great lengths in altering the constitutn. essentially were they allowed to give constructive powers to the Executive branch of the Govt.[42]

Smith's concern reflected his fear as a South Carolinian that legislative construction could lead Congress to interfere with the institution of slavery. His theory garnered only a handful of adherents.

Theodorick Bland of Virginia was the first to contend that executive officers should be removed in the same manner they were appointed, by the president "by and with the consent of the Senate." While agreeing that impeachment was a "supplementary aid favorable to the people," he insisted that it was "consistent with the nature of things, that the power which appointed should remove."[43] The debate on Bland's interpretation centered around the Senate's role as a check on the executive. Bland insisted that the Senate served as an executive as well as a legislative body.

Opponents of this theory feared the possibility of the Senate's sitting in judgment in a dispute between the president and one of his cabinet members. Perhaps Rep. Ames's speech best expressed this view:

> It will nurse faction; it will promote intrigue to obtain protectors and to shelter tools. Sir, it is infusing poison into the constitution; it is an impure and unchaste connection; there is ruin in it; it is tempting the Senate with forbidden fruit; it ought not to be possible for a branch of the legislature even to hope for a share of the executive power; for they may be tempted to encrease it, by a hope to share in the exercise of it.[44]

A majority of the representatives favored removal by the president alone, but they disagreed strongly over how the president obtained this power. Was it necessary for the legislature to grant this power to the president by statute or did the Constitution give him the power by implication?

Theodore Sedgwick of Massachusetts expressed some of the thinking of the members of the House who contended that the removal power must be granted by the legislature:

> The power of creating offices is given to the legislature: Under this general grant, the legislature have it under their supreme decision to determine the whole organization, to affix the tenure, and declare the control. This right of determining arises, not from express words, but by natural construction.[45]

Other supporters of this legislative grant theory believed the "necessary and proper" clause of the Constitution gave Congress the power to make any laws needed to carry the removal power into execution.

Those who contended that the removal power rested with the president through an implied constitutional authority argued that there was no need for legislation to affirm this authority. Ames strongly defended this viewpoint:

> The executive powers are delegated to the president, with a view to have a responsible officer to superintend, control, inspect, and check the officers necessarily employed in administering the laws. The only bond between him and those he employs is the confidence he has in their integrity and talents; when that confidence ceases, the principal ought to have power to remove those whom he can no longer trust with safety.[46]

Opponents greeted the exposition of this theory with alarm, contending that its acceptance would make the president a virtual monarch with absolute power over all the great departments. South Carolina's William Smith warned his colleagues not to be so dazzled by the virtue of the current president as to fail to see the dangerous precedents they established for the future.

Although the advocates of the constitutional grant theory lacked a clear majority in the House, their view eventually prevailed. This was because the majority saw removal as a presidential power and some proponents of the legislative grant theory were willing to accept any solution recognizing this. The debates reveal that members shifted their positions continuously. Even Madison, who originally had proposed the resolution granting the power by law, eventually defended the implied power argument.

In this theoretical debate, the members gave free rein to their creative oratorical talents. "Suppose the President should be taken with a fit of lunacy, would he not continue in office during his four years?" Rep. James Jackson of Georgia asked his colleagues. "Suppose the Senate should be seized, or the representatives themselves become lunatics, would not the people be obliged to submit to this mad Congress?"[47]

The first of the three executive department bills which the House sent to the Senate, the Foreign Affairs Act, contained no explicit language granting the president the sole power of removal. The Senate was divided on the issue even more than the House had been, and the debate was fast paced and colorful.

According to Maclay, Senator Oliver Ellsworth of Connecticut defended the language of the bill in an elaborate speech,

> drawn from Writers on the distribution of Government. the President was the Executive officer he was interfered with in the appointment it was true, but not in the removal. the constitution had taken one but not the other from him. therefore removal remained to him intire— he carefully avoided the Subject of impeachment— he absolutely used the following Expressions with regard to the President. *"It is Sacrilege to touch a Hair of his head, and, we may as well lay the President's head on a block and strike it off, with one blow".* . . . he paused put his hankerchief to his face and either shed tears or affected to do so.[48]

Most of the arguments of those senators who opposed granting the power to the president without requiring him to obtain Senate consent had been heard in the

House. In the Senate, opponents devoted more attention to the impact of the decision on the Senate's role and power. Maclay reported that they also noted the implications for federalism. "The Matter predicted by Mr. [Patrick] Henry, is now coming to pass," observed Antifederalist William Grayson of Virginia, "consolidation is the object of the New Government, and the first attempt will be to destroy the Senate, as they are the Representatives of the State legislatures."[49]

On the motion to strike the wording from the bill, the Senate's vote was tied. Vice President John Adams cast his deciding vote in favor of the president's ability to remove department heads without the consent of the Senate, an action for which he received much criticism.

This decision has had a profound effect on the evolution of the federal government. Giving further definition to the relationship between the president and Congress, it diminished the concept of the Senate as a quasi-executive body. Any similarity to the English ministerial form of government was avoided. Impeachment as a means of political control was prevented. It also marked the first use of the doctrine of implied powers.

Most importantly for those Federalists who supported a strong executive, the decision transferred more power to the presidency during George Washington's tenure. His unassailable reputation made him an invaluable asset to those who were working to achieve what they saw as a better "balance of power" between the legislative and executive branches. Opponents of a strong executive saw danger in this use of Washington's name. One of them worried about Washington's death as a melancholy possibility:

> if it should take place shortly, perhaps it would have been happy for america that General Washington had never been chosen. Relying on his virtue and abilities, congress have by law vested him with powers not delegated by the Constitution, which I suppose they would have intrusted to no other man— These powers cannot be recalled at any future period without the consent of his successor in office, or an union of Sentiment, which in these factious times, is not to be expected.[50]

Creation of the treasury department raised special concerns as it had under the Articles of Confederation. One question was whether the department should be headed by one person or a three person board. Elbridge Gerry of Massachusetts had led the successful fight in the Confederation Congress to replace the superintendent of finance with a three person board, but he failed in a similar effort in 1789. The new department would be headed by one person. Gerry complained to his old friend Samuel Adams, calling the bill the "most perfect plan I had seen for promoting peculation & speculation in the public funds."[51] Opponents predicted that if one individual held the responsibility without adequate checks, the position would prove too powerful. Again, the Federalists, seeking to develop a strong financial foundation for the nation, prevailed.

A second concern relating to the Treasury Act was whether its secretary should have a different relationship with Congress from that of the heads of other departments. Specifically, should he have the privilege of reporting to Congress in person

Congrefs of the United States,

BEGUN and held at the City of NEW-YORK,

On Wednefday the fourth of March, one thoufand
feven hundred and eighty-nine.

An ACT *to eftablifh the* TREASURY DEPARTMENT.

BE it enacted by the Senate and Houfe of Reprefentatives of the United States
of America in Congrefs affembled, That there fhall be a department of
Treafury, in which fhall be the following officers, namely ; a Secretary of
the Treafury, to be deemed head of the department, a Comptroller, an Auditor, a Treafurer, a Regifter, and an Affiftant to the Secretary of the Treafury, which Affiftant fhall be appointed by the faid Secretary.

And be it further enacted, That it fhall be the duty of the Secretary of the
Treafury to digeft and prepare plans for the improvement and management
of the revenue, and for the fupport of public credit ; to prepare and report
eftimates of the public revenue, and the public expenditures ; to fuperintend
the collection of the revenue ; to decide on the forms of keeping and ftating accounts and making returns, and to grant under the limitations herein
eftablifhed, or to be hereafter provided, all warrants for monies to be iffued
from the Treafury, in purfuance of appropriations by law ; to execute fuch
fervices relative to the fale of the lands belonging to the United States, as may
be by law required of him ; to make report, and give information to either
branch of the Legiflature, in perfon or in writing (as he may be required) re-
fpecting all matters referred to him by the Senate or Houfe of Reprefentatives, or which fhall appertain to his office ; and generally to perform all
fuch fervices relative to the finances, as he fhall be directed to perform.

And be it further enacted, That it fhall be the duty of the Comptroller to
fuperintend the adjuftment and prefervation of the public accounts ; to ex-
amine all accounts fettled by the Auditor, and certify the balances arifing
thereon to the Regifter ; to counterfign all warrants drawn by the Secretary
of the Treafury, which fhall be warranted by law ; to report to the Secretary
the official forms of all papers to be iffued in the different offices for collect-
ing the public revenue, and the manner and form of keeping and ftating the
accounts of the feveral perfons employed therein ; he fhall moreover provide for the regular and punctual payment of all monies which may be col-
lected, and fhall direct profecutions for all delinquencies of officers of the
revenue, and for debts that are, or fhall be due to the United States.

Treasury Act [HR-9], September 2, 1789
(Courtesy of the Connecticut State Library).

rather than in writing? Could he propose plans for legislation or should he be
confined to giving information? The issue was decided in favor of the duty "to digest
and prepare plans" and to "make report and give information to either branch of
the Legislature, in person or in writing, (as he may be required)."[52] By the second
session, Treasury Secretary Alexander Hamilton had submitted his report on the
public credit including draft legislation, i.e. "plans," to the Congress. During the
debate supporters of assigning the secretary the duty to report plans had argued
that he would not draft legislation.

The post office was seen as an executive function, but not one meriting a department. Nevertheless, establishment of a postal system proved difficult for the First Federal Congress. With the system created by the Old Congress in place, the adoption of permanent postal legislation was not attempted until the second session. During 1790 and 1791 three separate bills failed. The major point of disagreement involved the routes taken by the post roads and who would designate them. Since the post roads would become important economic arteries, local and sectional interests determined the members' positions. Bills that specifically delineated the routes the mail would take reached an impasse as members from the same and neighboring states fought among themselves. Legislation that would have avoided the problem by giving the power to the president died in the House. Congress eventually passed an act each session to continue the old system for a short period. The acts established the office of postmaster general, "subject to the direction of the president." In practice, the president delegated this oversight to the secretary of the treasury.

The appointment of a new postmaster general at the close of the first session caused a special problem for the Senate. He removed from office Mary Katherine Goddard, the popular deputy postmaster of Baltimore. Complaining that she had been removed from office without cause, she petitioned the Senate to reinstate her in the job. Dozens of prominent Baltimoreans, including Maryland's governor, signed a letter on her behalf, but were told that "some inferior offices would be put under the direction of the deputy here, & more travelling might be necessary than a woman could undertake."[53] Allegations that she was an Antifederalist sympathizer may have been behind the removal. She was not reinstated.

The Judiciary Act of 1789 created the position of attorney general, and assigned him the duty "to prosecute and conduct all suits in the supreme Court in which the United States shall be concerned."[54] He was also expected to serve as legal adviser to the president and heads of departments. The original Senate draft of the Judiciary bill called for the appointment of the attorney general by the Supreme Court. Eventually the Senate eliminated this provision and the bill, like those establishing the executive departments, fails to define how he would be appointed or removed. Perhaps the senators heeded the advice of individuals such as the Chancellor of New York, who wrote Ellsworth, "Is he not properly the representative of the executive of the state & to leave his appointment with the Judges is in some measure to blend him with the judicial."[55] The fact that the attorney general was responsible to the president, yet had judicial functions, is further evidence that the Federal Convention and the First Federal Congress saw the branches of the federal government as balanced and interrelated rather than completely separate.

In its legislative decisions taken in 1789 in relation to the so called "great departments," Congress accepted its responsibility for fleshing out and interpreting the Constitution. Critically important to the development of the executive-legislative relationship, these decisions still shape our government today.

the courts respectively, on motion as aforesaid to
give judgment against him by default.

And be it further enacted by the authority
aforesaid that suits in equity shall not be sus-
tained in either of the courts of the United States,
in any case where remedy may be had at
law.* ~~Nor shall deposition be admitted in either of said courts in suits in equity~~

And be it further enacted ~~by the
authority expressed~~, that all the said courts
of the United States shall have power to grant
new trials, in cases where there has been a
trial by jury, for reasons for which new trials
have usually been granted in the courts of
law. — And shall have power to impose &
administer all necessary oaths, & to punish
by fine or imprisonment, at the discretion
of said courts, all contempts of authority
in any cause or hearing before the ~~same~~,
& to make & establish all necessary rules
for the orderly conducting business in the
said courts, provided such rules are not
repugnant to the laws of the United States.

And be it further enacted by the authority

One page of the Senate draft of the Judiciary Bill [S-1], June 12, 1789
(Courtesy of the National Archives).

VI

Defining
the Federal Judiciary

I should consider the general Government as of very little consequence without its having a judicial co-extensive with its legislative power, & of equal energy; for of what avail are the wisest & most salutary Laws, without a firm & unbiased judicial, to carry those Laws into effect? (Rep. Abiel Foster of New Hampshire to Oliver Peabody, September 23, 1789, Chamberlain Collection, *Boston Public Library*)

While the House was occupied with the executive departments and revenue bills, the Senate's attention was focused on another organic act, the judiciary bill, legislation fundamental to the structure and development of the judicial branch of the United States government. Article III of the Constitution loosely outlined federal jurisdiction and gave Congress the authority to determine the number of justices on the Supreme Court and establish inferior federal courts. This Article has been called one of the major compromises of the Federal Convention, a compromise by postponement.

The Articles of Confederation had given the federal government jurisdiction only over causes arising on the high seas, boundary disputes between states, and conflicting land grants by different states. All other judicial functions were left up to the states. Consequently the Federal Convention lacked precedents to build upon. Delegates supported the creation of a Supreme Court and some understood that the high court would rule on the constitutionality of state and national laws, but viewpoints diverged, particularly on the subject of the inferior courts. Several delegates believed that such courts would infringe upon the jurisdiction of the state courts and compromise states rights. Practical politicians feared that including specifics on inferior courts would endanger ratification. After lower courts were struck out of the Virginia Plan, the delegates agreed to leave the decision on inferior courts to the Congress. Thus, the legislature held extensive formative powers over the judiciary and was required to answer the jurisdictional, structural, and procedural questions relating to the federal courts.

Despite this compromise by postponement, considerable controversy arose during the ratification debates and many expressed fears that federal courts would usurp the rights of the states. Many of the amendments to the Constitution proposed by the ratifying conventions sought to limit federal judicial power and protect individual rights in federal courts. Antifederalists also complained about judicial review. The most articulate on this issue was "Brutus," who observed that "the courts are vested with the supreme and uncontroulable power, to determine, in all cases that come before them, what the constitution means; they cannot, therefore, execute a law, which, in their judgment, opposes the constitution."[56] He disliked this because it allowed the courts to establish limits on the legislature.

Members of the First Federal Congress arrived in New York City well aware that the judiciary would be a major topic for their deliberations and that compromise would be necessary. In early April 1789 a committee consisting of one senator from each state represented at the time was appointed to prepare a judiciary bill. This committee met frequently for a month. On May 11, Maclay noted the formation of a subcommittee to draft a bill. When one considers the size of the full committee, the complexity of this legislation, and the lack of staff to draft it, it is not surprising that the committee resorted to the device of a subcommittee. Although this is the only one of two subcommittees actually mentioned in the documentary record of the First Federal Congress, subcommittees of one or two members must often have been employed for the purpose of preparing a working draft.

From the handwriting of the draft of the Judiciary Act, discovered buried away in the Capitol by historian Charles Warren in the 1920's and now in Senate Records at the National Archives, it is possible to conclude that two of the members of the subcommittee, which probably had three members, were Oliver Ellsworth of Connecticut and William Paterson of New Jersey. The handwriting also provides a clue about the work of the subcommittee, making it reasonable to surmise that the subcommittee divided the authorship of the bill, and each one concentrated on a particular area. Paterson authored the first nine sections, which established the structure of the court system. Sections ten through twenty-five, which relate to jurisdictional issues, were Ellsworth's creation. Section twenty-six is in the hand of Caleb Strong of Massachusetts, and suggests that Strong was the third member of the subcommittee. Unfortunately, in the only other piece of evidence, Strong did not admit to such a role. The remainder of the bill, in the hand of Benjamin Bankson, a Senate clerk, established procedures for the courts.

Annotations on the bill of amendments and new sections added by the Senate, together with Maclay's reports on the Senate debates, make it clear that Ellsworth was the main architect of the bill. He probably played a key role in the compromise which settled the issue that had troubled the Federal Convention by granting a degree of concurrent jurisdiction to the state and federal courts. He also authored the extremely important Section 25, which provided for final determination of constitutional questions by the Supreme Court of the United States. "This Vile Bill is a child of his, and he defends it with the Care of a parent," Maclay complained, "even with wrath and anger. He kindled as he always does When it was medled with."[57] Others, such as Rep. Abraham Baldwin of Georgia, were more complimen-

Senator Oliver Ellsworth
of Connecticut by James
Sharples (Courtesy
of Independence
National Historical Park).

tary toward Ellsworth: "The Senate have before them a bill on the judiciary department, in my opinion admirably contrived, my chum Ellsworth has been at work at it
night and day these three months."[58]

Once the committee had introduced the bill, the Senate ordered it printed. On
this legislation, more than any other, members of Congress sought advice from
constituents, especially attorneys and judges. This resulted in a second printing of
the bill because so many copies had been sent off for comment. Representatives
requested constituents' suggestions even before the bill arrived in that House.

Considerable advice was offered by those consulted. For example, a Virginian
warned James Madison that, "where there is danger of clashing jurisdictions the
limits should be defined as acurately as may be."[59] Fisher Ames thanked a friend for
his extensive comments, observing, "I am sure that you would not have been able,
with so many claims upon your time, to have criticised the principles of the bill so
closely, if the importance of the system to the well being of the Govt. had not made it
a favourite subject of reflection and study."[60] Senator Paine Wingate confessed to a
judge in his home state of New Hampshire that he supported the bill with reserva-
tions because "the administration of justice in the way proposed will cost more than
it is worth. The judiciary is calculated by pretty good judges to cost between 50 & 60
thousand dollars pr. annum & yet it will not extend to a tenth part of the causes

47

which might by the constitution come into the federal court."[61] Wingate's colleague in the House, Abiel Foster, informed a constituent after passage of the act that he had heard of uneasiness in New Hampshire about the bill, and wished "those politicians who are opposed to it, will be pleased to propose a substitute." He went on to counter several objections and state that he had "given my hearty concurrence to" it.[62]

The Senate debated the bill at length, exploring all its aspects: common law, chancery, the number of justices on the supreme court, jurisdiction, and jury trials. Knowing that in the future lawyers and judges would look to this legislation for guidance, they studied the implications of individual words and phrases. After eighteen days of debate, the bill passed on July 17 over the objections of six senators, two Antifederalists and four Federalists.

The House postponed the judiciary bill for a month while they completed the revenue system and considered Amendments to the Constitution. Taken up again in late August, the bill was put off a second time in favor of the debate on a bill to locate the federal capital city. When debate resumed, Sen. Morris noted that the many representatives who were lawyers kept "snarling at it" but expected that the House was "too Lazy & too Weak to make a bold Attack on it."[63] Morris proved correct. The bold attack never came, not even from Madison who was expected to fight the bill because of the problems it created for southern jurisprudence. The House debated the broad constitutional and political implications of the bill, but eventually left the Senate plan and its sometimes vague and open ended language intact.

Arguments against the establishment of inferior federal courts were articulated once more. Representative Aedanus Burke of South Carolina, a prominent member of the state bench, contended that such courts were unfair to American citizens. New Hampshire's Samuel Livermore and South Carolina's Thomas Tudor Tucker argued that they should be eliminated as too costly and an unnecessary interference by the national government in state affairs. Livermore even suggested that their establishment would lay the foundation for civil war.

Representative Theodore Sedgwick touched upon a major underlying issue when he declared that inferior courts were necessary to enforce the peace treaty of 1783. Under section twenty-five state laws and court rulings could be overturned if they conflicted with federal treaties, statutes, or the Constitution. The southern states, who owed most of the remaining debts to British creditors, recognized that the federal courts would force the payment of these debts, overruling decisions made by the state courts to forestall these payments.

The president signed the Judiciary Act of 1789 on September 24, thus setting the stage for the implementation of the third branch of the new government. Congress adopted several other bills relating to the federal judiciary or its functions. Except for the bill providing salaries, these bills originated in the Senate. Most important was the Punishment of Crimes Act, the first listing of federal crimes and their punishment. The Senate was unable to complete work on the bill during the first session, and the new drafting committee appointed in the second session simply reintroduced the earlier bill. In addition to treason and counterfeiting of federal records, the crimes included murder, disfigurement, and robbery committed in federal jurisdictions or on the high seas. This very explicit act authorized judges to sentence convicted murderers to surgical dissection after execution, and even provided fines and imprisonment for anyone attempting to rescue a body of an individual sentenced to dissection.

Members of Congress would probably have been amazed by the longevity of the system they established. At the time of the passage of the Judiciary Act even some of its supporters believed the establishment to be a temporary one that might need substantial alteration. In fact, before adjourning its second session, the House, in an attempt to regain some of the oversight of the judicial branch which it had relinquished to the Senate in 1789, ordered Attorney General Edmund Randolph to report on "matters relative to the administration of justice under the authority of the United States, as may require to be remedied."[64]

Randolph presented his extensive and complex report to the House at its third session. He aimed to separate as clearly as possible the jurisdiction of the state courts from the federal judiciary and his report included draft legislation outlining a complete revision of the Judiciary Act of 1789. One central provision would have curtailed the federal courts' ability to review cases tried in state courts involving questions of constitutionality. This was unacceptable to the Federalists. Recognizing the potentially devastating effect of Randolph's proposals on the federal judiciary, opponents made a gamble aimed at destroying them. Representative Egbert Benson of New York, who assumed leadership of the effort, proposed, as an alternative to the attorney general's report, a constitutional amendment for Congress to recommend to the states.

The amendment would have set up a General Judicial Court with original jurisdiction in all cases cognizable under Article III of the Constitution in each state. The states would appoint the judges, but Congress would pay them and regulate the proposed courts as it saw fit. The strategy was successful. Randolph's report and Benson's constitutional amendment, both of which had received widespread attention in the press, died in the Second Congress. Thus ended the threat to a strong federal judiciary.[65]

The Judiciary Act and the supporting legislation passed by the First Federal Congress established a strong federal judiciary with a system of inferior courts and appeals from them to the Supreme Court. At the same time the compromises made meant that the jurisdiction given was not as broad as could have been granted under the Constitution. The act brought to fruition the concept of a government composed of three branches and was so well constructed that substantial changes did not occur for a century. It remains the foundation of the federal judiciary today and ranks as one of the most outstanding achievements of the First Federal Congress.

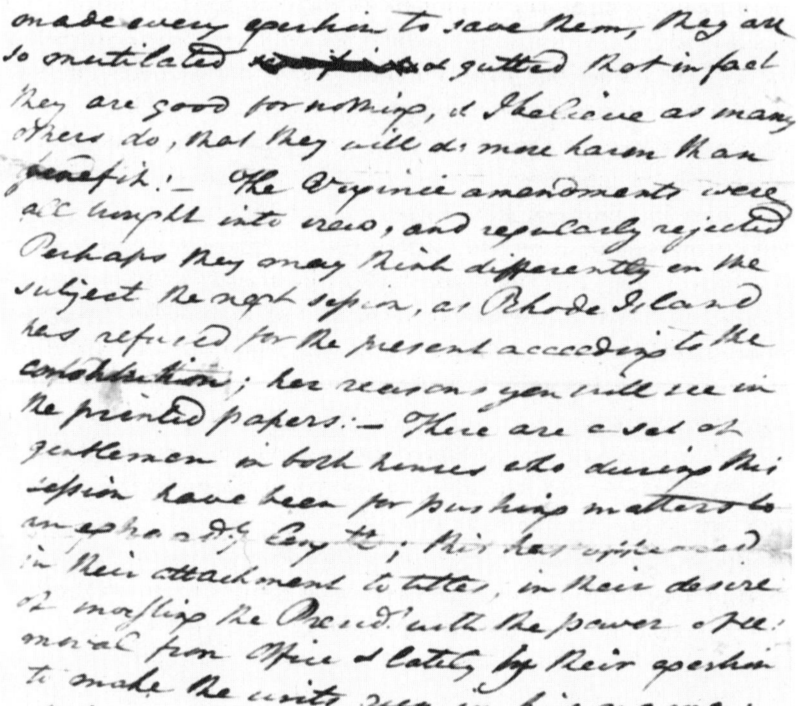

[Handwritten letter; partially legible]

made every question to save them, they are so mutilated ~~struck out~~ & gutted that in fact they are good for nothing, & I believe as many others do, that they will do more harm than benefit. — The Virginia amendments were all brought into view, and regularly rejected. Perhaps they may think differently on the subject the next session, as Rhode Island has refused for the present according to the constitution; her reasons you will see in the printed papers. — There are a set of gentlemen in both houses who during this session have been for pushing matters to an extraordinary length; this has appeared in their attachment to titles, in their desire of investing the President with the power of removal from office & lately, by their question to make the writs run in his name; their map in seems to have been to make up by construction what the constitution wants in energy. —

The Judicial bill has passed but wears so monstrous an appearance that I think it will be felo de se in the execution; the amendment of Virginia respecting this matter has more friends in both houses than any other, & I still think it probable that this alteration may be ultimately procured. — Whenever the Federal Judiciary comes into operation I think the pride of the States will take the alarm, which added to

Senator William Grayson of Virginia to Patrick Henry, September 29, 1789 (Courtesy of the Library of Congress). Senator Grayson, an Antifederalist, laments that opponents of the Constitution had accepted it with the expectation that amendments would be made, rather than insisting on amendments before ratifying.

VII

The Bill of Rights

Permit me then, with great respect to ask, Sir, how you can justify yourself, in the eyes of the world, for espousing the cause of amendments with so much earnestness? . . . . [people] regret particularly that Mr. Madison's talents should be employed to bring forward amendments, which, at best can have little effect upon the merits of the constitution, and may sow the seeds of discord from New-Hampshire to Georgia. ("Pacificus" [Noah Webster] to Rep. James Madison, August 14, 1789, *Papers of Madison*, 12:334-35)

Once Congress had adopted legislation for raising revenue and organized the executive and judicial branches outlined in the Constitution, its agenda became the question of amendments to the Constitution. At the Federal Convention George Mason of Virginia and Elbridge Gerry of Massachusetts had proposed that the Constitution include a bill of rights to reassure the people that the vastly strengthened federal government would not oppress them. The Convention refused unanimously. This proved a critical error, almost fatal to ratification of the Constitution.

During the contests over ratification of the Constitution and the first congressional election, the question whether the Constitution should be amended was at the forefront. The members of the state ratification conventions had proposed almost two hundred separate amendments, often as part of their official ratification document. Allowing for duplication among the proposals, about one hundred separate amendments emerged.

Most called for changes in the structure and powers of the new federal government. One of these declared as a principle of the Constitution a pure separation of powers among the judicial, executive, and legislative branches, with the latter dominant. Others, concerned with federalism and states' rights, aimed at altering the balance of power between the states and the federal government in the new system. Some southern Antifederalists sought amendments to give greater protection to sectional interests.

Amendments aimed at the judiciary proposed severe limitations on the jurisdiction of the federal courts; reliance on the state courts instead of establishing such inferior federal bodies as district and circuit courts; and appointment of presidential commissions to override unpopular supreme court decisions. Others sought to restrict the powers of the president by denying him a third term, establishing an accountable cabinet to advise him, and limiting his powers of pardon and command of American military forces in the field. Congress was also a target. Proposed amendments would have restricted its power to regulate state militias and federal elections, to exercise exclusive jurisdiction over the capital city, to adopt direct taxes and excises, to maintain a standing army in peace time, and to pass commercial laws. Most importantly, several states proposed that all powers not *expressly* or *clearly* delegated to Congress be reserved to the states.

Other amendments recommended by the states sought to provide protection at the federal level for certain traditional liberties claimed by Americans by virtue of their constitutional ancestry. Among these were freedom of speech, press, and religion; the rights to assemble, petition, and possess arms; and several provisions to protect Americans from an arbitrary judiciary.

Federalists generally opposed amendments on the grounds that the Constitution should be allowed a trial period for problems to show themselves. As to a Bill of Rights, they argued that one was unnecessary since most of the states had bills of rights, and the federal government created by the Constitution was a limited government which could not interfere with those rights. Antifederalists believed this argument to be naive, since the Constitution made the federal government supreme over the states. They insisted that amendments should be one of the first matters taken up by Congress. But Antifederalists fared poorly in the first congressional election. The likelihood that Congress would propose amendments dimmed.

Credit for the fact that the First Federal Congress proposed amendments to the states in September 1789 belongs to James Madison, who pushed them through a reluctant House of Representatives. At first as strongly opposed to amendments as other Federalists, Madison became a convert because of two factors: the arguments of his friend Thomas Jefferson and the antifederalism of his congressional district. By the close of 1788 he was persuaded that if Congress recommended to the states some amendments relating to personal liberty which did not alter the basic nature of the Constitution, most Antifederalists would be willing to support the new government. This would protect it from fundamental structural change. Madison converted Washington to his view. In his inaugural address, the president recommended that Congress consider amendments which strengthened "the characteristic rights of freemen."[66]

Madison first proposed that the House take up the question of amendments in May. A month later he presented several amendments which he believed should be woven into the text of the Constitution. Most were related to personal rights. One that was not, the one on reserved powers that became the Tenth Amendment, significantly omitted the words "expressly" or "clearly." The omission of this limiting word gutted the amendment and left interpretation of the Constitution open to the doctrine of implied powers.

Despite the fact that they held advanced civil libertarian ideas for their times,

Federalists in Congress were not as willing to consider amendments as Madison expected. They believed that the first congressional election had demonstrated that Americans were satisfied with the new government, and that considering amendments consumed valuable time that should be devoted to more pressing matters. Several went so far as to ridicule the value of paper declarations of rights. The handful of Antifederalists in Congress also expressed reluctance to consider amendments. They feared that the adoption of rights-related amendments would close the door to consideration of amendments designed to rein in the federal government.

When describing Madison's proposals, both Federalists and Antifederalists turned to the popular ship of state metaphor. They called them "a tub to the whale," a literary allusion to Jonathan Swift's *Tale of a Tub* (1704). In his story, Swift described how sailors, encountering a whale which threatened to damage their ship, flung it "an empty tub by way of amusement," to divert it. Madison's contemporaries used the allusion to illuminate the fact that he had proposed mostly rights-related amendments rather than ones designed to change the structure or essence of the new government. As a result, the Antifederal leviathan would be diverted and the ship of state could sail away intact.

Madison bristled at the allusion, but agreed to postpone the debate on amendments in order to complete the revenue system. At last in August he persuaded the House to consider the question. Antifederalists proposed several structural amendments, but Federalists defeated them one by one. In response to the Federalist argument that Americans did not support amendments, Aedanus Burke of South Carolina pointedly denied the observation frequently heard in the House, "That this revolution or adoption of the new Constitution was agreeable to the public mind, and that those who opposed it at first are now satisfied with it."[67] The heated debate, which included the first known instance of congressmen challenging each other to duels, presaged the conflict which lay ahead in September, when the House attempted to locate the federal capital.

The respect in which Madison's House colleagues held him gradually won support for the amendments from other Federalists, but at a price. They made several changes in his proposals. Perhaps most significantly among these they refused to accept his wish to add to the Constitution's preamble an eloquent statement, based in part on the Declaration of Independence: that all power comes from the people; that government should be exercised for their benefit, which he defined as "the enjoyment of life and liberty, with the right of acquiring and using property, and generally of pursuing and obtaining happiness and safety"; and that the people retain the right to change a government whenever it was adverse to or inadequate for the purposes of its institution.[68]

Madison also had to accept Roger Sherman of Connecticut's insistence that all amendments be placed at the end of the Constitution and not be woven into it. Thus, Americans owe to Sherman, actually an opponent of amending the Constitution, the existence of a separate group of amendments known as the Bill of Rights.

The Senate made further changes in the amendments passed by the House. Most significantly, it eliminated language that prohibited Congress from infringing the rights of conscience, declared separation of powers as a principle of the United States Constitution, exempted from military service those with religious scruples, and forbade the states from abridging certain rights of Americans. Madison, unhappy with the changes made by the House, was even more displeased by what the Senate did.

Congress sent twelve amendments to the states on September 28, 1789. Not until December 15, 1791 did the eleventh state ratify ten of them, modifying the United States Constitution for the first time. The three original states which had not ratified the amendments by 1791, Massachusetts, Connecticut, and Georgia, did so in conjunction with the sesquicentennial of the Bill of Rights in 1939.

Significantly, the necessary eleventh state in 1791 was Virginia, the home of George Mason, whose language in the Virginia Declaration of Rights of 1776 so influenced the federal bill of rights; of James Madison, whose persistence in Congress resulted in the adoption of the amendments soon known as the Bill of Rights; and of Thomas Jefferson, whose forward looking perspective recognized that the true importance of a Bill of Rights was "the legal check which it puts into the hands of the judiciary."[69]

VIII

Locating
the United States Capital

I had enough of it when I was in the old Congress and I see it is the same Pack of Cards shuffled and used for another Game. An odd Trick is often won I see by those who do not get the Rubber. If the Big Knife *[Virginia, and, in this case, George Washington] would give up Potowmack the Matter would be easily settled. But that you will say is as unreasonable as it would be to expect a Pennsilvanian to surrender at Discretion to New York. . . . It therefore amuses me to see the Arguments our grave politicians bring forward when I know it will be determined by local Interests which will not suffer Intrigue and Management to grow rusty for Want of Use. . . .* (Richard Peters to Thomas Jefferson, June 20, 1790, Julian Boyd, ed., *Papers of Jefferson*, 16:539)

In September 1789, as the first session drew to a close, Congress debated the divisive question of where it should establish its capital city. Because of the political and economic power the capital would bring to whatever locality, and particularly whatever section of the country, was chosen, the question had plagued the Confederation Congress since 1783 when several states invited it to locate the seat of federal government within their borders.

The New England States usually supported a site on the Delaware River near Trenton, which they considered to be central. The Southern States wanted a capital situated on the Potomac River, a location they believed would benefit the South's economy and its proportionate power in federal affairs.

In October 1783 the Confederation Congress voted to locate the federal town near Trenton. The southern congressmen reacted so violently that Congress quickly proposed that the United States have two federal towns: one on the Delaware and another on the Potomac near Georgetown, Maryland. This soothed southerners and provided the needed solution to one of the major sectional threats to the survival of the Union during the American Revolution. Despite the potential cost in money and time, the so-called dual residence plan had precedent in ancient confederacies and followed the practice of several northern states which did not have stationary capitals.

At the end of 1784 Congress repealed the dual residence resolutions and decided to build a single federal town on the Delaware River near Trenton. In the

Aquatint of a ferry on the Susquehanna River by William Strickland after
J. L. Morton (Courtesy of the Library of Congress).

meantime Congress would reside at New York City. The federal town was never
built because the Articles of Confederation required the votes of nine states to
appropriate money. Led by William Grayson, later a senator from Virginia in the
First Federal Congress, the South prevented any funding for the construction of the
federal town from being included in the 1785 federal budget.

The decision by Congress in September 1788 that the First Federal Congress
would meet in New York City angered both the Pennsylvanians and the southerners, who had supported Philadelphia as a more central choice. Banking on southern support, the Pennsylvanians planned to introduce a motion, as soon as the First
Federal Congress convened, adjourning it to Philadephia. When Congress did not
form a quorum in early March, the most talked about issue was the residence of
Congress. New Yorkers lobbied hard against the introduction of Pennsylvania's
motion, citing elegant Federal Hall as a prime reason for remaining in New York.
Fortunately for them, the Pennsylvanians had to abandon their plan when James
Madison refused his support. He feared a long debate that would interfere with
more urgent business. But to assuage the Pennsylvanians' feelings, he promised
consideration for such a motion at the end of the first session.

By the end of August several towns and cities had become competitors for the
prestige and economic growth associated with being the federal capital. The compe-
tition had intensified since the adoption of the Constitution. With the federal
government supreme over the states, Americans came to have a different view of the
place at which Congress sat. No longer would it be merely a federal town where the
federal government exercised some limited jurisdiction. Now it could be a one
hundred square mile federal district over which Congress would exercise exclusive

jurisdiction. Federal city and federal capital replaced federal town as the appropriate terminology.

The most northerly site proposed to the First Federal Congress focused on Trenton, but included land in both New Jersey and Pennsylvania. Federal City Road outside Trenton remains today a memorial to the proposal. Germantown and another area adjacent to Philadelphia offered themselves. So too did the Pennsylvania towns of Reading, Lancaster, York, and Carlisle. In Maryland, residents of Baltimore launched a publicity campaign on behalf of their city but did not petition Congress until the second session. The southernmost site to ask to be chosen as the seat of empire was Georgetown, Maryland, on the Potomac River. The several petitions which these towns and cities submitted to Congress included both detailed economic statistics and hyperbole to prove their merits. Promoters of the site around Trenton claimed the adjacent land was "capable of supplying Wood, as well for Fuel as for other purposes, by Water to the End of Time."[70]

As the session drew to a close the Pennsylvania delegation met several times to devise a strategy. Its members knew that neither the North nor the South wanted to change the temporary seat of government unless it was done in conjunction with determining the permanent seat of government. Pennsylvania faced a dilemma, whether to make a deal with the North to locate the federal capital in Pennsylvania after residing several more years at New York; or to negotiate with the South to locate the capital on the Potomac while Philadelphia immediately became the temporary residence. The Pennsylvanians decided on the former strategy. Early in September, Rep. Benjamin Goodhue of Massachusetts, acting on behalf of the states north of Maryland, proposed in the House that the capital be located on the Susquehanna River in Pennsylvania.

Led by Madison, a longtime advocate of a capital on the Potomac, southerners rose to the defense of that river. Feeling cornered by the uncompromising coalition facing him, Madison burst forth with an argument that reflected the beginnings of an important shift in his constitutional thought and in his role as leader of the Federalist party in the House. Despite southern passion and the threats of disunion voiced during the debate, the House passed a bill locating the capital on the Susquehanna River in Pennsylvania. The precise spot was to be selected by what would be the first presidential commission, but congressmen expected it to be near Wright's Ferry. That village lay on the east bank of the Susquehanna between Lancaster and York. A year before, the man who owned most of the land at the site had changed its name to Columbia in hopes of attracting Congress.

When Sen. Robert Morris of Pennsylvania had the audacity to ask President Washington for his opinion of the House decision, the "Great Personage" appeared even more reticent than usual.[71] He had good reason. If the Susquehanna bill passed Congress, he would have to pass judgment on it. Representative Richard Bland Lee of Alexandria hoped Washington would veto it as partial and unjust. So too did the president's closest confidant at home, Dr. David Stuart, the man whom Washington relied on to oversee his business interests in his absence. Stuart wrote the president anxiously from Alexandria, reminding him that the hopes of its

residents for a capital on the Potomac had always been centered on him. Circum-
spectly, Stuart suggested procedural grounds for a veto: the location of the capital
should not have been discussed without previous notice, nor before Rhode Island
and North Carolina rejoined the Union.

It was rumored that the southerners would filibuster the bill on the Senate floor.
This did not occur, and the first use of this parliamentary manoeuver was avoided.
Sen. Morris persuaded the Senate to amend the bill to place the capital so that it
would include Germantown, seven miles northwest of Philadelphia. When the
amended bill returned to the House, desperate attempts by the South to postpone it
failed. Finally, Madison turned to influential New Yorkers for assistance. He persuaded them to pressure their senators to help in postponing the bill until the next
session. Such a postponement would defeat at least temporarily a bill which rang the
death knell for New York City's tenure as the federal capital. The New York senators
agreed to support postponement if the bill returned to the Senate.

Madison then proposed a minor amendment which the House accepted. This
sent the bill back to the Senate and led to its postponement until the second session.
While some people thought that Madison had pulled the wool over the eyes of
northern congressmen, Rep. Fisher Ames indicated otherwise. Postponing a decision on the location for the capital, and remaining at New York, had been the
North's goal all along.

Much to the shock of the Pennsylvanians, Congress adopted a new rule when
the second session convened in January 1790: any business left unfinished at the end
of one session must begin anew, *de novo*, at the next. This precedent, which was
established specifically to kill the Seat of Government bill, remained a joint rule of
Congress for half a century.

Although the attention of Congress during the early months of the second
session was devoted to Alexander Hamilton's plans for funding the federal and state
debts, the issue of the location of the capital continued to bubble under the surface.
By mid May the Pennsylvanians and their allies in the Middle and Upper South
States had agreed to support the Pennsylvanians' proposal at the opening of Congress: removal to Philadelphia without first determining the location of the permanent capital. They were unsuccessful because of bitter opposition in South Carolina
and Georgia to residing at Philadelphia. The opposition of the Lower South arose
from the ease with which its members could reach New York compared with
Philadelphia and the anti-slavery climate of the Pennsylvania capital.

Instead, the South Carolinians and Georgians joined New York and most of the
New England states in supporting a new seat of government bill that contained
blanks in place of the names of the temporary and permanent seats. It was understood, however, that the strategy behind the bill was to keep Congress at New York
City. The congressmen committed to Pennsylvania's plan of moving to Philadelphia
without determining the permanent seat of government refused to vote "yes" for
any motion naming a place for the capital. This meant that no place proposed for
the permanent residence could obtain an affirmative vote.

Draft of the Residence Bill [S-12], May 31, 1790
(Courtesy of the National Archives).

By mid June the coalition favoring removal to Philadelphia without deciding on a permanent capital had been stopped in the House and the Senate, and the coalition that wanted to settle both issues together had been stymied in the Senate. At the same time, Alexander Hamilton's program for funding the national debt had not been enacted. It, too, was a question that inflamed sectional tensions and excited political passion.

No. 13.00A I Certify that there is due from the *United States* to *George Garland* the Sum of *Thirty pounds sixteen Shillings* viz.

For *his service as Sail & Tent maker from 1st Jan.ry to 31st March 1781 — 77 Days at one Dollar —*

	Dolls.	96ths.
	77	"
Total	77	"

Which Sum of *Thirty pounds Sixteen Shillings* shall be paid to the said *George Garland* or Order, in Specie, or other current Money equivalent, by the *first* Day of *May 1781* with Interest, at the Rate of Six *per Centum per Annum*, from the *first Day of May one thousand seven hundred & eighty one* until paid.

Witness my Hand, this *first* Day of *April*
A. D. 178*1*

Counterfigned.

Jno Tysson —

Tim. Pickering
Quarter-Mafter General.

Certificate issued by Timothy Pickering, Continental Army Quartermaster General, April 1, 1781 (Courtesy of the Museum of American History, Smithsonian Institution). The domestic debt consisted of a variety of fiscal papers issued by the Continental Congress during the Revolutionary War. Here the United States promises to pay George Garland $77.00 for his work as a sail and tent maker in 1781.

IX

Funding
the Revolutionary War Debt

Congress is daily engaged on the Report of Mr. Hamilton. I know no man in either house, who is not totally at a Loss on this important subject— Funding the debt is the word at present, but no one can tell wh. way it will end. Funding the debt may, or may not be, a blessing, or a Curse to the people of America, for ought I dare say, at present. But this I sincerely regret. It will add strength and power to that faction that brought about the late 2d. revolution, and it will make their princely fortunes. (Rep. Aedanus Burke of South Carolina to Samuel Bryan, March 3, 1790, Record Group 59, National Archives)

In the late eighteenth century the United States was an underdeveloped country with great potential for economic growth. The federal government could stimulate that growth if it could borrow money. This required that it have public credit, that is a good credit rating. To establish public credit the United States had to maintain a stable central government and convince its creditors that it could pay its huge revolutionary war debt. Recognizing this need, the Federal Convention had granted to Congress numerous powers so that it could regulate economic growth, but it had not specified the establishment of a particular type of economic system.

How to pay the debt had been a thorny economic and political issue for the United States after the war. The debt meant enormous power and became a major political issue between the states and the general government during the 1780s. This was because whichever level of government paid the debt would likely also possess the major taxing power and the allegiance of the people. It was intimately related to the question of federalism and remained so.

Americans supported payment of the foreign debt, but had different opinions about how to pay the domestic debt. Some proposed repudiation or scaling it down. Some believed it should be paid as quickly as possible by the sale of federal lands in the West while others supported a long term funding system which provided money to make regular interest payments on the debt until such time as the principal should be paid. Some men believed Congress should not pay the debt, but that it should be assumed by the states and paid by them. The latter idea was particularly anathema to those who favored a stronger central government, for the shared federal debt was a major force holding the loose Union together after the war.

In 1781 Congress appointed as its superintendent of finance, Robert Morris, later senator from Pennsylvania in the First Federal Congress. Morris believed that a public debt supported by federal revenue would prove an agent of commerce and the strongest cement possible for the Confederation. He called for existing federal debt securities to be exchanged for new securities, without a discrimination among original holders and purchasers of the debt certificates, and that interest on the debt be paid regularly from federal revenues.

Congressman James Madison took a leadership role in advocating the adoption of most of what Morris recommended, including no discrimination among holders of the domestic debt. In addition, Madison advocated that the federal government assume the state debts. In April 1783 Congress appointed three members to explain the plan to the states. All three would play a prominent role when the issue came before the First Federal Congress: James Madison, Alexander Hamilton, and Oliver Ellsworth. The failure of the states to ratify an amendment to the Articles of Confederation granting Congress a revenue, however, rendered the funding proposal academic.

The Constitution proposed by the Federal Convention provided in Article VI that "All Debts contracted and Engagements entered into, before the Adoption of this Constitution, shall be as valid against the United States under this Constitution, as under the Confederation." Massachusetts and South Carolina, both heavily burdened with debt, had argued that Congress be granted the power to assume the state debts. Hamilton, Madison, and others opposed the idea because they feared it would create opposition to the Constitution from those who would see state powers and rights further diminished.

Some Americans, especially those to whom the federal government was indebted, believed that provision for the public credit should be one of the first issues dealt with during the first session of the First Federal Congress. In their minds the public debt was the principal reason for the second revolution that had produced the new Constitution. Several prominent public creditors in Pennsylvania impatiently told Congress that it would be subjected to derision and reproach if action was not taken on the debt before the end of the first session. Declaring that a certain amount of debt could benefit the United States, they urged Congress to establish a long term funding system. Among other arguments, the petitioners observed that a funded debt would act as cement to strengthen and perpetuate the Union, binding the states to each other and the public creditors to the success of the federal government.

The House referred the memorial to the new secretary of the treasury, Alexander Hamilton, and asked him to report a provision for the support of public credit. Although several of his contemporaries had more experience in financial matters, Hamilton's appointment won wide acclamation. Federalist newspaper editor John Fenno described the new secretary as a man who "considers his fame as

Memorial of the Public Creditors of Pennsylvania, August 21, 1789
(Courtesy of the National Archives).

much at stake as ever a General of an Army did—and . . . wealth as less than nothing and vanity [when] contrasted with Honor & Reputation."[72]

Hamilton submitted his masterful report on the public credit to the House of Representatives on January 14, 1790. Recognizing the importance of the document, the House ordered 300 copies printed. It ran to 51 pages in length. Like Morris in 1782, Hamilton proposed to fund the debt. Funding related primarily to payment of the interest on the debt, not the principal; indeed he asked that no more than two percent of the principal be paid yearly. This meant creating from additional federal revenues a fund set aside to make regular and long term payments of the interest. To make the bookkeeping more manageable, new debt certificates would be printed to consolidate the various types of certificates issued during the Revolutionary War. In addition, Hamilton supported the assumption of the state debts, the creation of an excise to pay the costs of the assumption, and the establishment of a national bank. He opposed any discrimination between original and present holders of debt certificates.

Hamilton stated that by 1790 the federal debt had accumulated to more than $54,000,000. Of this, $11,710,378 was foreign debt, owed primarily to the French government and private citizens of the Netherlands. The domestic debt of $42,414,085 consisted of such fiscal paper issued by Congress as currency, interest arrearages, military pay and final settlement certificates, promissory notes for supplies, and validations for money loaned to the government. In addition, Hamilton estimated the war debts of the thirteen states at $25,000,000.

Hamilton's plan detailed why he thought the debt could be used as a national political and economic blessing. It would establish and maintain public credit thereby reviving confidence in the United States government both at home and abroad, tie the commercial and business interests as well as the state creditors to the success of the federal government, and better cement the Union together. It would also allow the federal government to leverage funds and form a partnership between the bank and the federal government to support the government and economic growth.

Congress began debate on the report on public credit on February 8. One New Yorker observed that New York City was "all in a flame about funding, nothing else heard even among the women and children."[73] The report met with quick endorsement from most members, but Madison led the opposition to two proposals. He favored discriminating between the original holders of the debt (for example, soldiers and those who had loaned Congress material or money) and holders who had purchased the certificates at less than face value. Also, he opposed the assumption of the Revolutionary War debts of the states into the federal debt.

By 1790 most of the debt certificates were no longer in the hands of those Americans who had actually loaned money or given services to the United States. This was because some Americans, particularly in the commercial North, saw speculation in state and federal debt certificates as a means of making more money much faster than in the respectable field of land speculation. The certificate market had become a growing business in the 1780s as speculators bought and sold for short term as well as long term gains. By 1787 most certificates were no longer in the hands of original holders. By 1790 almost eighty percent of all federal securities in Massachusetts had been transferred. Investors in the Netherlands held over two and a half million dollars of American fiscal paper.

Madison believed strongly that justice required that the original creditors should receive something, even if they had sold their certificates for far less than face value. He proposed on February 11 that holders of public securities originally issued to someone else—holders who were often castigated as speculators—receive the highest market value of such securities, and that the balance of the sum due from the public be paid to the original holder. Opponents of this discrimination saw it as an unconstitutional violation of contracts. The motion lost on February 22 by a vote of 36 to 13. As Senator Morris reflected after the second session closed, public credit was unpopular because "the many are to pay the few."[74]

The focus of the debate on Hamilton's report then turned to the assumption of state debts. The northern states were most heavily indebted and northern congressmen supported the proposal as vehemently as southerners opposed it. Heavily indebted South Carolina also supported assumption. Opposition arose from those who saw it as unconstitutional, a threat to state sovereignty, and perhaps a step toward the abolition of the states. Theodorick Bland of Virginia, an advocate for strong states, believed Hamilton's fiscal proposals would cripple the states: "Absorption of revenue will certainly follow Assumption of debt—so that our state governments will have little else to do than eat drinke and be merry."[75] Rather than support his longtime political enemy, Madison, Bland actually voted for assumption in the early stages of the debate, but died before the final roll call.

On April 12 the House defeated assumption, by the close vote of 31 to 29. William Maclay of Pennsylvania, Hamilton's most vocal critic in the Senate, was one of many interested people who observed the vote from the House gallery. None of the others however left so vivid an account of what happened. In a letter to a friend he summarized reaction to the vote: "Dismay seized the Secretary's Group. Speculation Wiped her Eye, and the Massachusetts men threatned a dissolution of the Union."[76] In his diary Maclay observed that:

> Sedgwick . . . pronounced a funeral Oration over it. he was called to Order, some Confusion ensued he took his hat & went out. When he returned his Visage to me bore the visible marks of Weeping. Fitzsimons reddened like Scarlet his Eyes were brim full. Clymer's color always pale now verged to a deadly White. his lips quavered, and his neither Jaw shook with convulsive Motions. His head neck & Breast consented to Gesticulations resembling those of a Turkey or Goose, nearly strangled in the Act of deglutition. . . . Ames's Aspect was truly hippocratic, a total change of face & feature. he sat torpid as if his faculties had been benumbed. Gerry exhibited the advantages of a cadaverous appearance. at all times palid, and far

from pleasing, he ran no risk of deterioration. Thro' an interruption of Hectic hems and consumptive coughs. he delivered himself of a declaration, That the Delegates of Massachusetts. would proceed no further, but write to their State for instructions. . . . Wadsworth hid his Grief Under the rim of a round hat. Boudinot's wrinkles rose into ridges. and the Angles of his mouth were depressed, and their apperture assumed a curve resembling an horse Shoe— Fitzsimons first recovered recollection. and endeavoured, to rally the discomfited & disheartened heroes. He hoped the good Sense of the House would still predominate and lead them to reconsider the Vote which had been now taken.[77]

On June 14, Oliver Ellsworth of Connecticut presented a resolution to include assumption in the funding bill which the House had sent to the Senate. On July 2 the Senate sent the resolution to committee. Ten days later the committee reported in favor of assumption, and on July 21, by one vote, the Senate attached assumption to the funding bill. Its inclusion resulted from the Compromise of 1790, by which Congress located the United States capital on the Potomac and assumed the state debts.

X

The Compromise of 1790 and Its Reaffirmation in 1791

The two great questions of funding the debt and fixing the seat of government have been agitated, as was natural, with a good deal of warmth as well as ability. These were always considered by me as questions of the most delicate and interesting nature which could possibly be drawn into discussion. They were more in danger of having convulsed the government itself than any other points. I hope they are now settled in as satisfactory a manner as could have been expected; and that we have a prospect of enjoying peace abroad, with tranquility at home. (George Washington to Marquis de la Luzerne, Aug. 10, 1790, Washington Papers, Library of Congress)

By the middle of June 1790, after five months of intense debate and politicking, Congress had made no final decisions in regard to either funding-assumption or the location of the capital. It had reached its first impasse under the new Constitution and legislative business almost stopped. The situation became so tense that Madison even considered forcing an adjournment of Congress so that passions could cool. Prominent men in both North and South began to question the viability of the Union and raise the possibility of civil war. American revolutionary leaders had cause to worry about the survival of the Union to which they had devoted their careers.

The South resented both its inability to establish the capital on the Potomac and the north's insistence that the federal government assume the state debts. Just after the seat of government debate in September 1789, one southerner concluded that if the conduct of the New England States and New York continued, Virginia should no longer look to the Union as the rock of salvation, nor consider whispers about separate confederacies as treason. The impassioned Henry Lee of Virginia (later to be the father of Robert E. Lee) complained bitterly. He asked his friend Secretary of War Henry Knox, whether, in light of the debate, the second revolution would produce half the benefits that had been predicted by supporters of the Constitution. In the spring of 1790 he flooded Madison with letters, concluding that he would "rather myself submit to all the hazards of war & risk the loss of every thing dear to me in life, than to live under the rule of a fixed insolent northern majority."[78]

Southern anger was fueled by the willingness of northern congressmen to discuss petitions against slavery and the slave trade during the early weeks of the second session. Great pains had been taken to prevent petitions against slavery from being submitted to the Federal Convention or the first session of the First Congress, but in February 1790 Quakers from Virginia, Maryland, Delaware, New Jersey, New York, and western New England called on Congress to regulate the slave trade. At the same time Congress received a petition from the Pennsylvania Society for the Abolition of Slavery, signed by its president, Benjamin Franklin. It asked Congress to use the powers inherent in the preamble of the Constitution to restore slaves to liberty, to "devise means for removing this *Inconsistency from the Character of the American People*," to "promote Mercy and Justice towards this distressed Race," and to "Step to the very verge of the Powers vested in you for discouraging" the slave trade.[79] Impassioned representatives from Georgia and South Carolina insisted that Congress lacked the authority even to discuss the petitions.

Before the vote against assumption on April 12, most public complaint with the federal government lay in the South. That vote evoked fundamental questioning of the new government among northerners. One of Rep. Goodhue's Massachusetts constituents reported to him that "people seem almost ripe for a national division of North & South. Perhaps it may be premature."[80] One disgusted Connecticut assumptionist, concluding incorrectly that the debate over the slavery petitions had caused southerners to oppose assumption, groused that Congress should "prefer the white People of this Country to the Blacks— After they have taken care of the former they may Amuse themselves with the other People— The African Trade is A Scandalous one, but let us take care of ourselves first."[81]

Few Americans had the perspective of Vice President John Adams, who feared that some of his "old friends both in Virginia and Massachusetts hold not in horror as much as I do a division of this Continent into two or three nations and have not an equal dread of civil war."[82]

With talk of disunion on the rise in Congress and the states, with the South and Pennsylvania fuming over the continued residence of Congress so far north, and with the North angry at the refusal of Congress to assume the state debts, a fundamental sectional compromise of almost constitutional magnitude appeared the only solution. In April and May congressmen and certain executive branch officials had sought to link the assumption and capital issues in such a compromise. They succeeded only in complicating and frustrating the legislative process as proposals for bargain after bargain were rumored, floated, or attempted.

The situation changed when Pennsylvania and the Upper South abandoned their strategy to consider only a temporary location for the capital. In early June when Alexander Hamilton, on behalf of the New Yorkers and New Englanders, proposed to the Pennsylvanians a capital-assumption bargain, by which Pennsylvania would get the permanent capital if it provided the votes needed for assumption. If this scheme succeeded, it would doom the dream of an American Empire centered on the Potomac. Consequently, Thomas Jefferson suggested that the

Representative Daniel Carroll of Maryland by John Wollaston (Courtesy of the Maryland Historical Society).

Pennsylvania delegation deal with the South instead. He proposed a permanent capital on the Potomac, following a long temporary residence at Philadelphia. Assumption of the state debts was not involved.

At the end of the week of June 13, during which the Senate had postponed both the capital and assumption questions, Jefferson ran into a distraught Hamilton in front of the presidential mansion. The latter raised the subject of assumption, stressing that New England considered it a *sine qua non* for continuation of the Union. Hamilton appealed to Jefferson to make common cause with him and bring success to the Washington Administration by seeking southern support for the measure. In response, Jefferson invited Hamilton and Madison to dine privately with him so that they might seek some resolution. Over dinner Madison agreed to provide the southern votes needed to adopt assumption, if Hamilton would use his influence with the New Englanders to prevent them from interfering with Jefferson's proposal to Pennsylvania for locating the capital on the Potomac.

Madison persuaded one senator and four representatives to change their positions on assumption. The wealthy Charles Carroll, whose twelve thousand acre estate lay just off the Potomac south of Frederick, Maryland, agreed to provide the necessary vote in the Senate. Two Virginia representatives with Potomac River districts promised Madison their votes: Alexander White, who represented Virginia

Political cartoon, July 1790 (Courtesy of the American Antiquarian Society).

from Harpers Ferry westward to the Ohio River; and Richard Bland Lee, who was told that the federal district would include Alexandria, the chief town in his congressional district. Two Maryland representatives did the same. Daniel Carroll represented a district which included Georgetown and all of western Maryland. George Gale, long a political supporter of the Potomac, resided on Maryland's lower eastern shore.

On his part, Hamilton asked the Massachusetts delegation, which spoke for New England's interests in Congress, not to interfere with the Philadelphia-Potomac capital bargain by joining in a counter offer to Pennsylvania. He also explained that it might be necessary for the state's senators to support the senators involved in the bargain on some votes related to the temporary residence. The Massachusetts delegation agreed to Hamilton's requests. Despite last minute attempts by New York's Senator Rufus King to arrange another bargain by which the capital would be located in Baltimore (after a few more years at New York), and the Marylanders would vote for assumption, the promise Hamilton had secured from the Massachusetts delegation effectively shut New York out of the decision making process.

On June 28 the Senate took up the postponed bill for locating the capital. An amendment by Charles Carroll, placing it on the Potomac between the Anacostia River and Conococheague Creek at Williamsport, Maryland, was adopted. The question of the location of the temporary residence brought on impassioned debate, but the Potomac-Philadelphia coalition prevailed with help from the Massachusetts senators, and the Senate voted to place it at Philadelphia. On July 1 the Senate passed the bill by one vote.

The House opened debate on July 6. Ripe rhetoric, dire predictions, and personal attacks entertained the packed galleries. In a reversal of his role in 1789, Madison led a majority which insisted that the bill be adopted without amendment; under no circumstances could it return to the Senate. On July 9 the House adopted the bill 32 to 29, and it went to Washington for his signature.

No one questioned the president's support for a Potomac capital. Nevertheless, he soon found himself confronted with appeals to, and attacks upon, his honor, particularly from the "betrayed" New Yorkers. On July 16 a newspaper described the president's situation as delicate, and observed that "bets are still open, at various rates"[83] as to what he would do. Washington stopped such speculation when he signed the bill that day.

For the first time Washington found his character attacked and himself publicly criticized for his actions as president. One newspaper writer referred to him as America's former favorite guardian and deliverer. Another declared that his ruling passion had been made clear by his signature. Several writers criticized the mayor and city council of New York for commissioning a portrait of Washington.

Soon after Washington informed the Senate that he had signed the bill, the senators added provision for the assumption of state debts to the House funding bill. The vote was 14 to 12 because Charles Carroll, as promised, changed his position. On July 24 the House agreed to assumption when Alexander White, Richard Bland Lee, Daniel Carroll, and George Gale joined the "aye" votes.

While the establishment of the capital on the Potomac and the assumption of state debts were the major components of the compromise of 1790, other related public credit issues were also resolved. Madison did not oppose the sinking fund which Hamilton proposed as a means of further indicating the federal government's intention and ability to pay its debt. Indeed, the bill creating the fund passed both houses the day it was introduced. Two other bills directly benefitted from the compromise of 1790: one settling accounts between the United States and the individual states and one raising new federal revenues to cover the cost of paying the interest on the state debt.

Some states had paid more to support the Revolutionary War effort than others and the Continental Congress had promised to equalize the effort. At the same time as it passed the bill funding the debt, the First Federal Congress passed a bill apportioning among the states the monies they had spent on the war effort. To benefit the South, where records were in some disarray, Hamilton agreed to liberalize the rules by which the states proved what they had spent on the war.

Hamilton wanted an excise act levying new taxes on imported spirits and on domestic liquor stills to cover the increased interest payments which resulted from assuming the state debts. "Among the expected glories of the constitution, next *to the abolition* of *Slavery* was that of rum, but melasses has shipwrecked New England virtue," Rep. George Clymer of Pennsylvania observed after the tariff debate of 1789 to fellow signer of the Declaration of Independence Benjamin Rush. "We must look to a day Still more distant for the promised blessing—some hope there is however that a congressional excise will reach the distillations."[84]

The College of Physicans of Philadelphia, of which Rush was an active member, seized the opportunity presented by Hamilton's proposal to attack what it believed was the tendency of Americans to drink too much alcohol. Its petition to Congress, which Clymer presented, asked for "such heavy Duties upon all distilled Spirits, as shall be effectual to restrain their intemperate use in our Country." If the federal government heard a rumor of a plague that could kill thousands of Americans, the government would surely take vigorous measures to combat it. "Your Memorialists can see no just cause, why the more certain and extensive Ravages of distilled Spirits upon human Life, should not be guarded against with corresponding Vigilance and Exertions."[85]

The House adopted the so-called excise act in January 1791. Madison, Carroll, Lee, and White were virtually the only southerners to vote for the bill. Although the amount of the duties did not satisfy some of those who sought to restrain drinking, many Americans protested against them. The act led in 1794 to the Whiskey Rebellion, in which the federal government first employed military force to impose its will on disobedient citizens.

Influential national leaders saw the compromise as the only means of preserving the Union and urged public support for it. Northern leaders proclaimed assumption—and the acceptance of the constitutionality of implied legislative powers on which it was based—to be the final cementing of the Union and downplayed the implications of a southern capital. Southern leaders heralded the decision to place the capital on the Potomac and stressed those provisions in the funding act which most benefitted the South.

Americans and supporters of the new nation residing in Europe made perceptive comments about the Compromise of 1790. From London, Gouverneur Morris observed that even though the site chosen was not good, the establishment of a single permanent capital enhanced the importance of the federal government. At Caen, France, Hector St. John de Crevecoeur once again turned his attention to the future of the United States. Eight years earlier, as "An American Farmer," he had published one of the first analyses of the American character. To him assumption meant that the Union had been consolidated, and the "Great Revolution began in '87" under the influence of American reason accomplished. He predicted American "Industry will assume More Expanded Wings, commerce, agriculture, the usefull arts will progress on with double Speed;" and that "the Hints Printed some Years ago by an Insignificant Scribbler called the Am. F. will be Justified by the Event; he was then called an Enthausiast because he foresaw the Good Sense of the Americans would lead Them Right at last."[86]

The Constitution survived its first major crisis because the American public was willing to accept the compromise worked out by the executive and legislative branches of the federal government in 1790. The first publicly fought out compromise in American history, it marked the end of the American Revolution, for it resolved the two most difficult and lingering issues: what to do about the war debt and where to locate the capital. Thirty years later, in 1820, and thirty years after that, in 1850, northerners and southerners again reached fundamental compromises which preserved the Union. Ultimately compromise failed, and the civil war which some Americans had discussed in 1790 took place.

New Yorkers complained bitterly about the compromise. Abusive articles treating Congress and the president more harshly than ever before filled the newspapers. Political cartoons circulated on the streets of the city in July. One showed Sen. Robert Morris, led by the devil, en route to Philadelphia with Federal Hall on his shoulders. A Philadelphia prostitute promised pleasure ahead, as did a man in women's clothing who identified himself as Congress's procuress. Another cartoon accused Washington of having self-gratification at heart when he signed the bill placing the capital on the Potomac.

The third session of the First Congress met at Philadelphia in December 1790. The Philadelphians had considered erecting a new building for Congress on one of the undeveloped squares west of Broad Street. Instead they provided the Philadelphia County Courthouse, which had been built between 1787 and 1789. Only minor changes to accommodate its new purpose were made in the building, which was renamed Congress Hall. The House Chamber took up most of the first floor while the second floor consisted of the Senate Chamber and several offices. Pennsylvania provided additional space in the State House, or Independence Hall, just to the east. Congress Hall, which was greatly expanded in 1793, still stands.

A week after the third session of Congress convened at Philadelphia in December 1790, southerners saw what some thought might be the first legislative threat to a removal to the Potomac in 1800: Alexander Hamilton's plan for a national bank. They believed that the federal government and the bank would quickly become so entwined that one would hardly be able to get along without the other. The bank would make Philadelphia, already the financial capital of the United States, also its permanent political capital. All the attempts of Madison and his southern supporters to defeat the bank bill failed. Whenever Madison exhausted other avenues, he would scour the Constitution in search of some grounds for declaring a bill unconstitutional. He raised such a contention about the bank bill at the last minute, claiming the Congress had no power under the Constitution to charter a bank. His opponents considered the argument merely a smokescreen for his real interests, and the bill passed Congress by substantial majorities.

The South's only hope lay in persuading the president to use his veto power for the first time. Washington, whose desire to protect the federal city against any threat faced its first test, shared their concern. He turned immediately to his attorney general and secretary of state for opinions on the constitutional question. The two

Congress Hall and the New Theatre, Chestnut Street, Philadelphia by
William Russell Birch and Thomas Birch (Courtesy of the Library Company
of Philadelphia).

Virginians deemed the bill unconstitutional. Washington sent both opinions to
Hamilton for his arguments in favor of its constitutionality.

In the meantime Washington had issued a proclamation announcing the site he
had chosen for the federal capital. Washington not only included his home town of
Alexandria—south of the lower limit specified in the act of 1790—but also named a
point within the town as the starting place for the survey of the district's boundaries.
In a letter to Congress, the president asked for a supplemental act so he could
complete the federal district to his liking, by taking in both Alexandria and land
south of the Anacostia in Maryland. Several congressmen privately expressed shock
that Washington had sent the divisive issue of the location of the capital back to
Congress. Washington had enough faith in the compromise of 1790 to take the risk,
but he would have to pay an unexpected price.

As Washington considered vetoing the bank bill, Maryland Sen. Charles Carroll introduced the bill the president had requested. The Senate postponed it for
one week, to the very day by which Washington must have either signed or vetoed
the bank bill. The first confrontation between a congressional majority and a

74

president over a possible veto loomed. By the morning of the tenth day there was general uneasiness and the president "stood on the brink of a precipice from which had he fallen he would have brought down with him much of that glorious reputation he has so deservedly established."[87] Washington signed the bill, and the Senate immediately adopted the postponed bill allowing him to include Alexandria in the federal district. The House agreed to it without comment. (In 1846 the United States retroceded to Virginia that part of the District of Columbia which lay south of the Potomac.)

The third session of the First Congress, at which it reaffirmed the compromise of 1790 reached during the second session, "passed with unusual good temper. The last was a dreadful one. In public, as well as in private life, a calm comes after a storm."[88]

Representative George Clymer of Pennsylvania by Charles Willson Peale
(Courtesy of the National Portrait Gallery, Smithsonian Institution).

XI

"Westward the Course of Empire Takes Its Way"

The Western Country is daily moving into greater importance, and many Members of Congress are not sensible of its Consequence to the United States, perhaps untill they now met, they never had occasion to bestow a thought upon it. Proper Attention to that Country is Absolutely Necessary, in time it will give Law to America. (Adam Stephen to Rep. James Madison of Virginia, September 12, 1789, *Papers of Madison*, 12:398)

Leaders of the American Revolution, such as Benjamin Franklin, John Adams, and George Washington, had been profoundly influenced by the mid-eighteenth century historical thesis, "Westward the course of empire takes its way," from Babylonia across the Mediterranean and Europe to North America. They believed that the United States was destined to become a vast republican empire, the largest empire ever known. It would include not only all the land between the Atlantic and the Pacific oceans but also that from the Arctic Ocean to the Isthmus of Darien (Panama) and the islands of the Caribbean. By 1789 the United States already spanned the middle of the North American Continent from the Atlantic to the Mississippi River.

In that year Jedidiah Morse justified publication of his popular *American Geography* on the premise that "we cannot but anticipate the period, as not far distant, when the AMERICAN EMPIRE will comprehend millions of souls, west of the Mississippi." Not all Americans thought settlement of the West would, or should, come rapidly. With the public divided on the issue, the First Congress moved cautiously as it initiated a military and Indian policy, admitted new states, and sought a way to sell off its vast holdings of virgin land.

Southerners saw the West and the new states it would produce as a key to future southern control of the federal government, for both they and the New Englanders believed that any future western states were more likely to unite politically at the federal level with the South than with New England. Southerners frequently complained that Congress did not appreciate the importance of the West and in fact took every opportunity to throw obstacles in the way of western settlement. They raised concerns that if the West were not nurtured it would unite with Spain or Great

Britain, whose colonies bordered it, or perhaps even establish itself as an independent nation.

Madison sympathized with the needs of the West and he assured correspondents soon after the First Congress met that he did not expect it to enact legislation purposely injuring the West. Indeed he hoped for a policy of active support, the key to which lay in empowering the executive branch to defend western interests. By the close of the first session however Madison had become extremely alarmed for the West. He saw New Englanders as raising fresh objections to western settlement on the expectation that it would separate from the original states.

Despite Madison's fears, New Englanders in Congress divided over the question of the West. Some, such as the senators from Rhode Island, saw it as essential to cementing any viable union between the North and South, for it would be in the West that the people and customs of those two diverse sections would mingle. To John Adams, whose political and diplomatic career had wed him to the idea of an expansive American empire, no questions about retaining the West as part of the Union existed. Indeed he used the West as one argument in his campaign to endow the president of the United States with a "royal title." Without the respect inherent in a title, a popularly elected president could never maintain his authority over a widely extended empire.

Other northerners however feared the potential alliance between future western states and the South. Southern congressmen worked hard to convince them of the importance of the West, even suggesting that if the United States proved too large and diverse to remain united, the division of territory should not be between East and West, but between the states north and south of the Hudson River.

In particular, southerners worked on Rep. Fisher Ames, who had quickly established himself as the spokesman for New England's interests in the First Congress. They had assistance from the West, for New Englanders had actually been the first settlers in the Northwest Territory. Members of the Ohio Company, both at Marietta and at home in New England, pressured Ames to attend to western needs. In July 1789 he responded by asking Ohio Company leader Rufus Putnam how the West could be retained as part of the United States, and of what use it would prove to the nation. Putnam argued that it was certainly in the West's interest to remain in the Union, but also that the Union would benefit financially from the sale of western lands and from the revenue duties raised there. It would be far less expensive for the United States to support a small army to control the Indians than to protect a border with an alien nation if the United States, despite western wishes, forced the West out of the Union. Putnam's lengthy response converted Ames, and he declared that Congress should "manifest a fixed resolution to protect the most remote parts of the union—to nurse the weak and to console the suffering remote settlements, with a degree of tender solicitude proportioned to their defenseless condition. . . . Our Sun will set when the Union shall be divided."[89]

Despite the contention of Rep. Elias Boudinot of New Jersey that "the Western Country blossoms like a rose & affords a happy Assylum for all the oppressed of the

Dear Sir.

A bill now before our house to regulate the sale of the back territory, like all others of the kind, giving emigration "lighter wings to fly", brings this evil more home to my feelings — This fatal propensity might at all times be opposed with effect by truth and reason, but truth and reason are not always obvious to common apprehensions, and on this subject above all others, there are some who pretend even to think it stand in need of being enlightened. Were I in the habit of addressing the public a pamphlet should come out entitled "The folly of emigrating to the western lands demonstrated" — I would endeavour in familiar language to shew to the meanest capacities that this desire proceeds either from the neglect of calculations or bad calculations. I would go deeply into the comparison of advantages between making a settlement on the western waters and those on the Atlantic — A particularity of facts on this point would seize the senses more strongly than any general reasoning however good. — I would prove lands producing for the Atlantic

Representative George Clymer of Pennsylvania to Benjamin Rush, August 7, 1789 (Courtesy of Richard H. Kohn, George Curtis, and Kenneth R. Bowling). The strongest statement against immediate settlement of the West came from Rep. Clymer of Philadelphia.

Earth,"[90] the most vocal and public antagonism to the West's rapid settlement came from the Middle States. In August of 1789 Rep. George Clymer of Philadelphia urged publication of a pamphlet to demonstrate the folly of emigrating to the West. He believed that the fatal propensity of Americans to move westward could at all times be opposed by truth and reason, but that such arguments mystified the limited capacities of the Americans most likely to consider the move. The pamphlet should be written in familiar language to convince men of such capacities that they would never succeed until such time as the gradually "extending circle" of civilization reached the West.[91] Clymer held to his anti-western view so adamantly that in the debate over funding the national debt in April 1790 he declared it entirely romantic to believe that the West would remain part of the Union. Congress should not consider it, its present population, or its vacant lands in the decision making process.

Clymer had been motivated in his suggestion by the debate in July 1789 on opening an office to sell public lands. Rep. Thomas Scott of western Pennsylvania proved to be an able if hyperbolic advocate of such an office. The West was of immense future consequence to the United States and its needs should be attended to immediately, he argued. History since the time of the Garden of Eden showed that empire had been slowly but invariably moving west. The impetuous current settling the West could not be stopped, but Congress could control it in the best interests of the nation, thus forming an empire illustrous and extensive.

Despite Scott's eloquence, the First Federal Congress could not overcome the division of opinion among its members about the importance of the West and the mechanics of selling lands there. Indeed, the West would have played a much smaller role in the First Federal Congress had the executive branch not repeatedly raised the issue.

Although his inaugural address had given no hint of the leadership role that he would assume, from May 1789 until the close of the First Congress Washington regularly submitted substantive messages on matters demanding legislative attention. More than eighty percent of these related to western issues, particularly Indian affairs and the military establishment. Washington focused attention on the West because he believed it vital to the national interest as well as because his personal interest in the area was both deep and long standing.

In addition to the firm prodding from the executive branch, senators and representatives felt pressure from western settlers. "Our ardent Wishes are such as will never admit the Idea of Separation unless you on the East Side compel it," a resident of Marietta wrote to Senator Oliver Ellsworth of Connecticut. "We therefore ought to be attended & fostered as a feverish child."[92] In another example of such lobbying, a Kentuckian advised House members from Virginia that "An augmentation of the army will no doubt be necessary. And the beginning of a Navy." He suggested a line of garrisons along the border between American and Spanish territory.[93]

During June and July 1789, Secretary of War Henry Knox made an extensive report to the president on the Indian situation in the West. Knox pointed out that, while treaties had been made with all the Northwest Indians except those along the Wabash, hostilities between some members of those tribes and the western settlers threatened the peace with other tribes. Arguing that decisive action was necessary to prevent general hostilities with all the Indians northwest of the Ohio, he presented the president with two courses of action.

The first would be to use military force to remove the refractory tribes completely. Knox then proceeded to make an eloquent statement in favor of a different choice:

> The Indians being the prior occupants possess the right of the soil—It cannot be taken from them unless by their free consent, or by the right of conquest in case of a just War—To dispossess them on any other principle would be a gross violation of the fundamental Laws of nature, and of that destributive justice which is the glory of a nation.[94]

Ironically, these noble sentiments, which included regret about the extinction of several tribes before the middle of the eighteenth century, were followed immediately by an admission that the United States government at the time possessed neither the financial nor the military resources to accomplish the suggested military goal. In reality, the military option was not a viable choice.

The House of Representatives quickly responded by choosing the second option: appropriating funds for negotiations with both the Wabash Indians in the Northwest and the Creeks in Georgia. But the Senate halved the amount appropriated, and focused upon the negotiations with the Creeks as the priority issue, putting resolution of conflicts with the Indians along the Wabash on hold.

In August Washington asked Congress for a statute to conform the existing military to the Constitution. The legislative history of the Troops Act reveals the first steps taken by the new government to authorize military operations on the frontiers. Before Congress acted on the president's request, it received yet another message, this time requesting a temporary provision for calling out the militia of the states. Washington acted in response to an urgent letter from the Governor of the Northwest Territory, Arthur St. Clair, who envisioned authorization to call up the militia as a means of conciliating western settlers and intimidating the Indians. The bill passed by the House stated specifically what state militias could be called up and limited the numbers in each state, but the Senate amended it to give the president substantially more power to deal with the situation.

The first session ended with Congress having followed the president's lead on all matters relating to Indian and military policy. During the second session, the process of building a federal military establishment would begin in earnest, and further steps down the path to an Indian war would be taken.

In his January 1790 state of the union message Washington stressed the need for Congress to direct its attention to providing for the common defense, citing preparedness for war as one of the most effectual methods of preserving peace. He also transmitted a report from Secretary of War Henry Knox. Justifying a proposed doubling of the number of federal troops, Knox called the current force completely inadequate and outlined the objects of the military establishment: to prevent the usurpation of the lands of the United States, to facilitate the surveying and selling of the same, and to protect the frontiers from Georgia to Lake Erie. As in 1789, Knox, after restating his frustration with the retaliatory measures taken by the settlers and his belief that the Indians retained their right of soil in areas not ceded in treaties, again expressed his hopes for negotiating an end to hostilities with both the Creeks and the Wabash Indians and gave Congress an estimate of the cost of such negotiations.

Senator William Maclay predicted: "give Knox his Army, and he will soon have a War on hand. indeed I am clearly of Opinion That he is aiming, at this even now." Maclay took particular exception to the title of the legislation, "An Act for regulating the Military Establishment of the United States." He proposed changing it to state the exact purposes of the military augmentation as listed in Knox's report. Believing that the "Constitution certainly never contemplated a Standing Army in time of peace," Maclay and others wanted to limit the establishment both in its purposes and its length of existence.[95] They failed to change the bill's title, but did push through an amendment reducing the size of the increase over the old establishment by fifty percent. Another bill, authorizing $20,000 for treating with the Indians to complete the talks with the Creeks and negotiate with the Indians on the Wabash, was approved.

During the first few months of the second session, Congress also had before it Knox's detailed and, at the same time, philosophical report, A Plan for the Militia of the United States. It called for universal male military training and recommended federal policy for running summer training camps in locations distant from urban vices. Knox saw militia training as a way to shape the moral and patriotic fiber of the nation and encourage republican virtue.

With Knox's report as a starting point, a House committee drafted a militia bill, but the legislation was not considered. Instead, the bill was ordered printed with the understanding that it would lie over until the next session while members solicited public opinion. This rather unusual move indicated the sensitive nature of the legislation, particularly its removal of the militia from state control and the issue of who should be exempted from militia service. It was a wise decision on the part of Congress, for nothing it considered raised as much organized public opposition as Knox's militia plan.

Besides holding public meetings to discuss the bill, individuals and groups petitioned Congress. Quakers complained about having to pay for their exemption on the grounds of conscience. A manufacturer sought to add glass workers to the list of exempted occupations. During the unsuccessful attempt to adopt a militia bill in the third session, southerners took the opportunity to castigate the Quakers for their behavior during the Revolution.

At the same time, a newspaper reported a fictitious conversation among several ladies who expressed concern about the effect on members of Congress of all the groups interested in the bill. One lady feared that the pressures might make some of them return home "crack-brained or hysteric." Recognizing that the militia bill had been stalled in part by petitioners demanding exemptions, another lady proposed that young women "learn militia duty, and turn out with both musquet and bayonet." A third welcomed militia duty because:

> We shall in this western hemisphere set up a FEMALE EMPIRE . . . [I] hope that we have 100,000 sisters in the United States. I anticipate the glorious day when American ladies shall be Commanders, Presidents of Congress, Ambassadors, Governors, Secretaries of State, Professors, Judges, Preachers. . . .[96]

Washington and Knox soon decided that they could not wait for Congress to organize the militia before beginning a military expedition. Since 1789, a steady stream of vivid letters and depositions describing attacks on Americans by renegade members of tribes along the Wabash had flowed into Knox's New York City office. The process of negotiating treaties with these tribes continued, but Knox believed that just the reports of such attacks on settlers would alarm the whole frontier and damage the government's reputation. In June 1790 he sent orders to launch an expedition against the offending Indians.

When the third session of the Congress opened in Philadelphia in December of 1790, the first rumors of the action that had occurred in October 1790 were circulating. Eventually, Congress received official news that 183 federal troops and militia had been killed, almost double the Indian casualties.

Congressmen received letters of protest which intensified their own misgivings. A constituent asked how the people of Connecticut could be persuaded that it was all right to sacrifice two white soldiers for every Indian. Senator Paine Wingate of New Hampshire decried the cost of the expedition, both in money and men, and lamented: "We have been told that the late expedition was successful; but the truth is, it has stirred a hornets nest in that country which we do not know what to do with."[97] On the other side of the question, westerners expressed the desire for a second expedition "without which our frontiers must inevitably become a Second time a wilderness."[98]

Knox and Washington pressed Congress for the authority to create, and funding for, an additional regiment of regular troops. With the request came stacks of supporting materials, including the numerous vivid reports of the Indian depredations that had led Knox to order the expedition. Although the House again debated the issue in secret session, it is clear that the drafting and passage of the legislation authorizing a new regiment was not a rubber stamp for the executive's request. Perhaps the regrets of Congressman Nicholas Gilman of New Hampshire best reflect the opinions of members who feared the effects and expense of an Indian war: "It is perhaps a misfortune that we have any connexion with that Country— I fear it will prove so in the end but we are now so involved that under present circumstances there seems to be no retreat."[99]

View of West Point, New York, by J. Smillie from original etching by Pierre L'Enfant (Courtesy of the State Historical Society of Wisconsin).

In the end, Congress gave in to the pressure from the executive and the western settlers by agreeing to the further augmentation of the federal troops. This large scale expansion of the federal military, and the open hostilities between the United States and the Northwest Indians, took place despite the fact that many congressmen doubted that the United States could govern and protect the West and feared the potentially destabilizing influence of westward expansion on the original states.

Secretary of the Treasury Alexander Hamilton also played a part in the pressure the executive placed on Congress. During the Revolutionary War the United States had fortified Stephen Moore's land at West Point on the Hudson River in New York and had continued to occupy it. In May 1790 Moore petitioned Congress for compensation. Hamilton, to whom Congress referred the matter, called West Point vital to the defense of the United States and declared that when the public interest required the use of private property, its owner should be compensated. On July 5 Washington signed an act authorizing the purchase.

The First Federal Congress did pass several laws relating to the West without prodding from the executive. Besides the land office bill, it took the initiative on provisions for surveying public lands, for estimating the amount of unclaimed western land, and for settling the claims of the settlers at Vincennes, Illinois.

Most importantly, during the first session Representative Thomas Fitzsimons of Pennsylvania called for legislation declaring the Northwest Ordinance to be federal law under the Constitution. Why this particular Ordinance of the Confederation Congress and not dozens of others? To fulfill a promise dating back almost a decade and to resolve a question the Federal Convention could not. In

August 1787, just after the enactment of the Northwest Ordinance by the Confederation Congress, Gouverneur Morris of New York proposed eliminating the provision in the draft Constitution which allowed new states to be admitted to the Union on an equal footing with the original thirteen on the Atlantic coast. Morris succeeded and the Constitution is silent on this issue. In August 1789 Washington signed the Northwest Territory Act, reaffirming the statutory validity of the Northwest Ordinance, which provided equal status for new states. When it admitted Kentucky and Vermont to the Union in 1791, Congress not only gave them equal status but also established the precedent that for each new southern state a northern one would be admitted and visa versa.

Despite its ambivalence towards the West, the First Federal Congress clearly put the might of the federal Government behind the idea of empire. Indeed, the word "Ohioisms," a term used by some contemporaries to demean the West and its boosters, never found its way into the American lexicon.

List of american Prisoners at algiers 9th July 1790,
with the Sums demanded by the Regency for their Ransom.

Crew of the Ship Dolphin captured 30th July 1785.

Richard O'Bryan	Captain. Ransom demanded £	2,000
Andrew Montgomery	Mate	1,500
Jacob Tessanier	French passenger	2,000
William Paterson	Seaman (keeps a Tavern)	1,500
Philip Sloan		725
Peleg Lorin		725
John Robertson		725
James Hall		725

Crew of the Schooner Mary taken 25 July 1785.

Isaac Stephens	Captain	2,000
Alexander Forsyth	Mate	1,500
James Cathcart	Seaman (keeps a Tavern)	900
George Smith	(in the King's House)	725
John Gregory		725
James Hermet		725

algerine Zequines 16,475

Duty on the above Sum 10 p Ct 1,647½

Sundry Gratifications to Officers of the Dey's Household and Regency, equal to 17½ Zt each Person . . . . . . } 240½

34792 281/30 Mexican Dollars @ 38 mozunas each are Zequines . . } 18,362½

List of ransoms demanded for American citizens held hostage in Algiers
(Courtesy of the National Archives).

XII

The Senate
and Foreign Policy

Depend Honoured Sirs, that it is Very Prejudicial to any Nation that Leaves their Subjects in Slavery—for in no one Respect Can it be any advantage to the Country they belong to—for the greater the time They are in Slavery—the Greater Difficulty in Releaseing them & it is well known that the price of Slaves is Riseing on Every application. (Captain Richard O'Bryen, a hostage in Algiers, to the Congress of the United States, July 12, 1790, Senate Records, National Archives)

The framers of the Constitution divided the conduct of American foreign policy between the president and Congress. The House must approve all appropriations. The Senate was assigned a more intimate role. By a two thirds vote, it must give its advice and consent to all treaties. The first Senate considered several matters relating to foreign affairs and indian treaties sent to them by President Washington. Although the Senate Executive Journal never indicates when an issue was debated, the proceedings illustrate that the Senate took its responsibility seriously, giving full consideration to each request for its advice and consent.

The first two times Washington sought the advice and consent of the Senate on such matters, for the Treaties of Fort Harmar and the Consular Convention (with France) of 1788 negotiated by Thomas Jefferson, it was for completion of projects launched before 1789, and he communicated with the Senate through the Confederation Congress's secretaries of war and foreign affairs. A Senate committee recommended approval of the treaties of Fort Harmar two months after they were referred to them. Nearly another month elapsed before the Senate gave its consent. In the case of the Consular Convention, which defined and established the functions and privileges of French consuls in the United States and American consuls in France, the Senate first requested a translation from John Jay, and then his opinion as to its fidelity. They asked Jay to supply all papers relating to the negotiations, and eventually ordered him to appear before them to answer questions and give his opinion as to whether the treaty should be ratified. After receiving Jay's assurance that the Consular Convention should be approved, they assented.

The first time that Washington desired the Senate's advice on how to proceed with negotiations he did so in person. Accompanied by Secretary of War Henry Knox, he came before the Senate to report on the status of hostilities and treaties with the southeastern Indian tribes and to obtain the Senate's answers to questions relating to the positions the federal government should take in future negotiations. While treaties existed with the Cherokee, Choctaw, and Chickasaw nations, the Creeks had refused to negotiate.

Senators clearly found themselves in an uncomfortable spot. The president obviously expected their immediate consent. Vice President Adams began to put the questions in the president's message to a vote as soon as the report had been read. Senator Maclay rose to voice his objections: "The business is new to the Senate, it is of importance, it is our duty to inform ourselves as well as possible on the Subject. I therefore call for the reading of the Treaties and other documents alluded to." Eventually, Sen. Robert Morris moved to commit the report in order to give the Senate time for consideration and discussion. The President "started up in a Violent fret. *This defeats every purpose of my coming here.*"[100] Both sides compromised when they agreed to postpone the issue to the following Monday, rather than commit it. The president returned to the Senate on that day to complete the business, but did not consult the Senate in person again. This set a precedent that continues today.

As a result of the Senate's advice, a commission negotiated with the Creek nation but had no success. Washington dispatched a special envoy to invite the king of the Creeks, Alexander McGillivray, to come to New York and negotiate. McGillivray, who was one fourth Creek, had assisted the British during the Revolutionary War and allied his tribe with the Spanish when the British departed. He was fully confident of his own ability to negotiate face to face with the president of the United States. He arrived in New York on July 22, 1790 with an entourage of thirty warriors. An observer described the grand manner in which the United States government received a foreign head of state for the first time. After the King of the Creeks had visited Washington at the presidential mansion on Broadway, he went to the residence of New York's Governor. McGillivray was then "paid great honor" as he "hookd Arms with The Secratary at war Hugh [Henry] Knox and Colon. Humphrey" and walked through the streets. At the Battery they "smoked the Calumet of peace & as they went through the Streets they Sung a Verry peculiar Song. . . ."[101]

A single commissioner, Henry Knox, was designated to meet with the Creek leaders. Before long it became clear that McGillivray and the Creek nation required a guarantee of access to American ports in case Spain should close its Florida ports to Creek trade. Washington consulted the Senate about making such a guarantee but omitted the fact that the secret articles named McGillivray as the commercial agent of the United States in the Creek Nation, with the rank of brigadier general and pay of twelve hundred dollars annually. The Senate's reaction to the secret articles which effectively granted McGillivray a monopoly is unknown, since Maclay had gone home in anger the day after the Senate voted to assume the state debts.

William Maclay's description of Washington's visit to the Senate on August 22, 1789 (Courtesy of the Library of Congress). William Maclay's diary contains a wealth of information on the first Senate and politics in the First Federal Congress.

The Georgia legislature was so outraged by the treaty that while it officially agreed to abide by its terms, it censured several articles. At this point Georgia was still unaware of the secret articles.

The president consulted the Senate on two matters concerning relations with Great Britain. First, he responded to a complaint from the State of Massachusetts regarding encroachments on its northern (Maine) boundary by British citizens in Nova Scotia. The Senate gave very general advice that "effectual Measures should be taken as soon as conveniently may be to settle all Disputes with the Crown of Great Britain relative to that Line."[102]

Washington also took the initiative in commercial relations, another area of conflict with the nation's former enemy. After the conclusion of the first session, he secretly delegated Gouverneur Morris to question British leaders informally on this subject. Morris's mission was to ascertain whether the British contemplated a commercial treaty with the United States, and convey in general terms American conditions for such a treaty. Washington warned Morris not to lose sight of the fact that, "the privilege of carrying our productions in our Vessels to their Islands, and bringing in return, the productions of those Islands to our own ports and markets, is regarded here as of the highest importance." The envoy was also instructed to inform the British that their conditions for removing their troops from the Great Lakes Forts had been met, and "it is natural to expect, from the assurances of his Majesty and the national good Faith, that no unnecessary delays will take place."[103]

Morris, while he succeeded in communicating the American position, failed to conclude an agreement. When the president finally informed the Senate of the existence of this secret diplomatic mission, he justified it by claiming the United States would be "less committed" because Great Britain would be talking with "a private rather than to a public person."[104] Maclay saw the president's message as evidence that the president had used his influence to defeat the discrimination in favor of French vessels during the debate on the Tonnage Act in the first session. A French protest against this act lay before the Senate at the same time as they first were told of the unsuccessful advances to Great Britain. Maclay contended that Washington "did it to facilitate a Connection with Great Britain. thus offering direct offense to France and incurring the Contempt of Britain,"[105] and went on to predict a war with the British. No further action was taken on this issue during the First Federal Congress.

The first Senate also confronted an international situation in which American citizens were being held hostage. When Congress convened, several American citizens, who had been taken off the ship *Dolphin* and the schooner *Mary* in July of 1785, were being held captive in Algiers. One of the hostages, Captain Richard O'Bryen, represented the group in communicating with the United States government. O'Bryen pleaded with Congress to ransom the hostages, saying that the plague had wiped out a large number of slaves and thus the ransom had gone up: "Be assured Honoured Sirs, that if the Terms is not Complyed with, that we are the Most Wretched & Miserablest Slaves in the world, for we shall be Doomed in perpetual Slavery."[106] Through intermediaries negotiating for the United States, the rulers in Algiers stated the ransoms demanded for the captives. The president brought the hostage matter to the attention of Congress in December of 1790. On February 1, 1791, the Senate resolved that forty thousand dollars should be appropriated for the ransom, but on March 3 a new resolution rescinded this action, citing the unexpected cost of the expedition against the Indians in the Northwest Territory.

By the time the release of the hostages was negotiated, many more American citizens toiled as slaves in Algiers and several had died of the plague. The government finally paid a lump sum ransom and agreed upon an annual tribute at a total cost of nearly one million dollars. In 1797, eighty-two hostages arrived in Philadelphia to a joyous welcome. Ironically, Richard O'Bryen was named American Consul in Algiers. Enslavement of Americans and the question of paying tribute ceased in 1815 after the United States attacked the Barbary States.

Rep. Fisher Ames of Massachusetts by Gilbert Stuart (Courtesy of the National Portrait Gallery, Smithsonian Institution).

XIII

Political Parties
in the First Congress

The seeds of two contending factions appear to be plentifully sown. The names of federalist and antifederalist are no longer expressive of the Sentiments which they were so lately supposed to contain; and I expect soon to hear a couple of new names, which will designate the respective friends of the National and particular [states rights] Systems. The People are very evidently dividing into these two parties. (John Quincy Adams to John Adams, April 5, 1790, Adams Family Manuscript Trust, Massachusetts Historical Society)

An unexpected result of the First Congress was the strides which that body took on the road toward political parties, institutions not recognized in the Constitution. Americans have always been a fractious people and throughout the Revolution they divided into parties and factions in their town meetings and in state legislatures. In Congress it had been the same since the clash between advocates and opponents of independence. Once the party favoring independence had won, delegates in Congress divided over the question of American federalism: how much power should the states delegate to the central government? That debate began in 1776 and culminated in the debate over the Federal Constitution in 1787 and 1788. But it did not end there.

The political parties which evolved during the 1790s originated in the House of Representatives. They were deeply rooted in the familiar debate over federalism. As the First Congress convened in March 1789, James Madison predicted "contentions first between federal and antifederal parties, and then between Northern and Southern parties."[107] He proved correct on both accounts, although before the parties appeared the First Congress enjoyed a four month respite from political factions.

The consensus among Federalists of all regions of the country which carried the Constitution to ratification and swept its supporters into the First Congress carried over into its deliberations. Trouble was expected in April and May when the House debated a revenue system. Senator Paine Wingate of New Hampshire observed that "there was sometimes suggested a jealousy respecting the different interests of the Northern & Southern states. But they were kept out of sight as much as possible."[108]

No one could restrain Georgia Representative James Jackson in his passionate defense of southern interests. In early June South Carolina Rep. William L. Smith wondered how long the spirit of harmony could continue in such a large body composed of men of "such jarring interests coming from such different countries and climates and accustomed to such different manners."[109] He would not have long to wait.

The first crack in the consensus came in June when the House implemented Article II of the Constitution. Antifederalists were strong advocates of legislative control of the executive and they found allies among the Federalists. In the tense debate on the power to remove executive officials from office, House Speaker Frederick A. Muhlenberg feared the creation of an Antifederal monster. But Rep. Ames later reported that the "sparks of faction" from the debate "went out for want of tinder."[110] Some Federalists supported Rep. Elbridge Gerry's attempt to place control of the treasury in a board rather than in a single individual. After losing that fight, the same representatives attempted to insert language into the Treasury Act which made clear the subservience of the secretary of the treasury to the House.

In mid July Ames expressed his suprise that, "To whatever cause it may be owing, the fact is certain, that there is very little of party spirit in our house, and less seeming intrigue and cabal than I have ever seen in any public body."[111] Yet he recognized three classes of troublemakers who could be strong when united: the Antifederalists, the dupes of local prejudice who feared New England influence, and the violent republicans "who would not make the law, but the people, king . . . who are more solicitous to establish, or rather to expatiate upon, some high-sounding principle of republicanism, than to protect property, cement the union, and perpetuate liberty."[112] John Fenno, editor of the *Gazette of the United States*, agreed with Ames that as yet no parties had formed, but wondered how long this could continue. Neither man would have recognized the House six weeks later.

In August came the debate between Federalists and Antifederalists over whether to add amendments to the Constitution altering the internal structure of the new government and the balance of power between the states and the federal government. Antifederalists, even with the support they found from Federalists, made no headway. Tempers rose with the temperature. Speaker Muhlenberg declared it the most heated discussion yet, and predicted intense debates for the remainder of the session. Indeed, he thought the sooner the first session adjourned the better.

The situation worsened considerably. With a federal revenue system in force, the executive and judicial branches of the new government established, and structural amendments defeated, the Federalist consensus had achieved its major constitutional goals and proceeded to split along sectional lines. The issue which caused the rift and escalated tension and party spirit to their first session apogee was the question of the location of the federal capital city. Regional interests prevailed as a majority coalition of New England and Middle States congressmen supported a site on the Susquehanna River in Pennsylvania. Led by Madison, the southern minority advocated the Potomac.

Feeling cornered, Madison responded with a lengthy and startling speech; startling not only for its content, but also for its bitterness and emotionalism, elements previously absent from Madison's speeches. The Virginian accused the North of denying the South its right to a free and open debate on the issue, and claimed his state might not have ratified the Constitution had it been able to foresee such high handed oppression. Federalists and Antifederalists alike must have been suprised when they heard Madison use the phrase "Confederacy of States" in place of "Union" or "nation" and his defense of the interests of the states. Even more shocking was his acknowledging some validity in the Antifederal argument that the territory of the United States was too large for a republican government to survive.

At the end of the session, Senator Grayson of Virginia wrote Patrick Henry that the members would have left New York City "in a tolerable temper" had it not been for the altercation over the seat of government. It "left very strong impressions on the minds of the Southern gentlemen. They suppose, with too much reason, that the same kind of bargaining which took effect with respect to the Susquehanna may also take effect in other great national matters." This could "be very oppressive to a defenceless naked minority" and "gentlemen now begin to feel the observations of the Antis, when they informed them of the different interests in the Union & the probable consequences that would result therefrom to the Southern States, who would be the milch cow out of whom the substance would be extracted."[113]

Concern mounted in the South in the wake of the capital debate. When southern congressmen returned to their districts after the first session, they found significant unhappiness with Congress. With time to reflect, Madison began to reconsider his position on federalism. His answer to Alexander Hamilton's request for advice on his plan for the support of public credit illustrates the change well. Madison separated himself from former Federalist allies like Hamilton, advocating rapid extinction of the debt rather than prolonging or perpetuating it in a funding program. Perhaps, he concluded, "some of the ideas I have hazarded may proceed not only from an inaccurate view of the subject but from a mistake of local for general sentiments with regard to it."[114] Hamilton might well have translated this to mean that Madison's position was not rigid and would be strongly affected by local opinion. The secretary knew the force that local opinion had had on Madison when he surprised many Federalists by his strong advocacy of amendments to the Constitution during the first session.

In the second session, Madison's leadership of those representatives who sought to discriminate among holders of the public debt and who opposed federal assumption of the state debts shocked Hamilton and many northerners in and out of Congress, who had turned him into a national hero. Rep. Theodore Sedgwick of Massachusetts considered him "an apostate from all his former principles. Whether he is really a convert to antifederalism . . . or whether he means to put himself at the head of the discontented in America time will discover."[115] By the end of the session Madison's colleagues had stripped him of his informal position as leader of the House Federalists.

The division over assumption was North versus South. By June northern anger

Representative James Madison
of Virginia by John Trumbull
(Courtesy of Mrs. Arthur Iselin
Collection, Frick Art Reference
Library).

over the failure to assume the state debts was matched by southern anger over the failure to locate the capital on the Potomac. Looking back on his thirty years of public service, Senator Richard Henry Lee observed: "It is impossible, for me to describe the scene here . . . every thing met with in my former life is mere trifling, compared with this, and you know that I have been in very stormy legislative scenes."[116]

The Compromise of 1790 which resolved these two issues made for a less rancorous third session, but sectional tensions remained. The South was less satisfied with the compromise than the North. The Virginia legislature had even gone so far as to declare assumption unconstitutional. Sectional tensions grew worse as Congress debated the excise and bank bills.

Intertwined with sectionalism were the issues of states rights, limited versus broad construction of the Constitution, and federalism. "Already we begin to perceive the collision of the Government of the United States with that of the individual States," observed Georgia Senator William Few, who found too many public officials ready "to augment and extend the powers of the former over the ruins of the latter. Some indeed have imbibed the idea that nothing but a consolidated Government will answer the purposes of general protection and safety." These men, Few continued, pursued "with avidity all such measures as tend to that object, notwithstanding they may be an obvious violation of the principles And genius of the Constitution." They defended themselves by "what is termed the sweeping clause, which they contend gives the United States all powers that they may think necessary to exercise for the general interest and safety."[117]

As the third session neared its end, Madison's leadership of the southern and states rights interest in the House caused a former admirer to state that he had degenerated into "the insignificant leader of an impotent Minority."[118] The minority would not long be impotent. But long before it became a majority, Madison would not be its leader. In fact, even before the First Congress adjourned, Thomas Jefferson had begun to assume leadership of what would eventually be known as the Democratic-Republican Party. His flurry of letters to southern Federalists and Antifederalists, and particularly to New York Federalist Robert R. Livingston, sought to expand the base of the party which Madison had led in Congress. Jefferson asked Livingston if the people in New York were as contented with the proceedings of the new government as their congressional delegation reported, and informed him that "there is a vast mass of discontent gathered in the South."[119] When Jefferson received Livingston's answer confirming northern discontent, he was launched on his career as an opposition party leader.

Madison continued to lead the party in Congress, as it expanded its base and effectiveness, but it made sense for Jefferson rather than Madison to be seen as the party's head and its presidential candidate. Jefferson, known as the author of the Declaration of Independence, was untainted by a leadership role in the Federalist Party during the debate over the Constitution. In fact, he had been in France, far from the clash of issues. Rep. Ames observed what he thought were Jefferson's presidential ambitions as early as the January 1791 congressional debate on a bill providing for the presidential succession.

The opposition party which emerged during the First Federal Congress would place Jefferson in the presidency at the same time as the federal government moved its capital to the Potomac. His victory deeply disturbed Fisher Ames, the leading spokesman for both the North and the Federalist Party in the First Congress. When Ames died on July 4, 1808, the old Federalist Party which had implemented the Constitution during the First Federal Congress died with him. The issue of federalism and the conflict between North and South remained.

Conclusion

The third inst. closed the political career of the first Congress of the United States, under the new Constitution: As a skilful pilot, after he has conducted the vessel, committed to his charge, through straits, abounding with rocks, quicksands, and shoals, and has given her a fair offing to the port of destination, experiences indescribable sensations of pleasure, so our political fathers may congratulate themselves on the success of their endeavors in conducting our political affairs through paths before untried. From this auspicious period, may they behold the labours of their hands maturing to a happy state of perfection. It is a pleasing reflection, that their administration has been so far to public acceptance, as to secure the re-election to office of a great majority of their number: In several instances, a re-appointment has been voluntarily declined—and those who have lost their re-election, are not without reflections to counter-ballance the disappointment. (Philadelphia, *Pennsylvania Journal*, March 9, 1791)

As soon as the First Federal Congress completed its work, historians as well as journalists began to analyze as well as praise its achievements. Jeremy Belknap hoped that, after twenty-five years of controversy and Revolution, the nature of the federal government had been happily settled.[120] Concluded a widely reprinted newspaper article as the third and final session of Congress convened, "The establishment of the federal government completed the revolution of America." Its author, reflecting the Federalist bias of the newspaper which originated the piece, editorialized that "before this event, it was problematical whether our emancipation from the sovereignty of Britain, would prove a curse or a blessing."[121]

As the third session drew to a close, congressmen realized that time would prevent final action on some bills in contemplation. "We leave unfinished the Post Office, the Militia and the Mint," Rep. Alexander White reported, "but on a Review of what we have done, and the manner it has been done in the course of two years—I think we may return to our Countries [states] without a Blush."[122] Senator Joseph Stanton explained to the Governor of Rhode Island that "Different Laws, Customs, and Habits of thinking have heretofore prevailed in the States which now Constitute the American Nation." Consequently, it was not surprising "that in forming, digesting and bringing to Perfection those Systems . . . which are to pervade the Empire and to extend to every individual Citizen some difference of Sentiment should prevail." It was these differences of opinion to which Stanton attributed the inability of Congress to complete its legislative agenda.[123]

In addition to the three bills which Rep. White mentioned as not completed by the First Congress, four other matters were left unresolved: creation of a land office, establishment of a pension program for disabled veterans and the widows and orphans of revolutionary soldiers, taxation of the slave trade, and provision for presidential succession. The Second Federal Congress, almost two-thirds of whose members had served in the First Congress, agreed to legislation on all of this business except the slave trade, a matter left to the Third Congress. Despite these postponements, the achievement of the First Federal Congress was awesome, especially considering that ninety-five men did it without staff or standing committees and at a total cost, including salaries, travel, printing, supplies, and wood for their fireplaces, of less than $374,000.

If the members of the First Federal Congress "do not retire with a loud clamour of universal applause, they may receive sufficient consolation from the general happiness, which they have diffused over our Country," a friend wrote Vice President John Adams, who must have taken pride in the letter's laudatory summation of the accomplishments of Congress. "In no nation, by no Legislature, was ever so much done in so short a period for the establishment of Government, Order, public Credit & general tranquility."[124]

Notes

1　Ebenezer Dibblee to Samuel Peters, November 16, 1787, Peters Papers, Church Historical Society, Austin, Texas.

2　James Madison to Thomas Jefferson, February, 14, 1790, Charles Hobson and Robert Rutland, eds., *The Papers of James Madison* 13:41.

3　Jonathan Elliot, ed., *Debates in the Several State Conventions on the Adoption of the Federal Constitution . . . .* (5 vols., Philadelphia, 1861), 4:222.

4　*Gazette of the United States* (New York), June 24, 1789.

5　Gordon DenBoer and Lucy Brown, eds., *The Documentary History of the First Federal Elections, 1788-1790* 2:45.

6　Merrill Jensen and Robert Becker, eds., *The Documentary History of the First Federal Elections, 1788-1790* 1:657.

7　James Madison to Samuel Johnston, June 21, 1789, *Papers of Madison* 12:250.

8　William Few to Governor Edward Telfair, June 20, 1789, Telfair Papers, Georgia Historical Society.

9　Paine Wingate to President Josiah Bartlett, January 26, 1791, Dartmouth College Library.

10　Robert Morris to Gouverneur Morris, March 4, 1789, Rare Book Room, Cornell University.

11　William Maclay to Jared Ingersoll, July 4, 1789, Maclay Diary Manuscript, Vol. 1, Library of Congress.

12　As reprinted in *Independent Gazetteer* (Philadelphia), February 3, 1789.

13　Edward Bangs to George Thatcher, [January, 1791], Thatcher Papers, Boston Public Library.

14　*Morning Post* (New York), March 14, 1789.

15　Frederick A. Muhlenberg to Benjamin Rush, March 5, 1789, Gratz Collection, Historical Society of Pennsylvania.

16　Elias Boudinot to Hannah Boudinot, May 15, 1789, Boudinot Family Papers, Rutgers University.

17   *Cumberland Gazette* (Portland, Maine), March 19, 1789.

18   Fisher Ames to William Tudor, April 1, 1789, Massachusetts Historical Society *Collections*, ser. 2, 8:316.

19   George Washington to Marquis de Lafayette, January 29, 1789, Washington Papers, Library of Congress.

20   James Madison to Edmund Randolph, March 1, 1789, *Papers of Madison* 11:453.

21   Fisher Ames to George Richards Minot, April 4, 1789, Seth Ames, ed., *Works of Fisher Ames* (2 vols., Boston, 1854), 1:33.

22   Benjamin Huntington to Governor Samuel Huntington, March 11, 1789, Samuel Huntington Papers, Connecticut Historical Society.

23   Fisher Ames to George Richards Minot, March 25, 1789, *Works of Ames* 1:31; William Maclay to Benjamin Rush, March 26, 1789, Rush Papers, Library of Congress.

24   Samuel Huntington to William Samuel Johnson and Oliver Ellsworth, March 30, 1789, Johnson Papers, Connecticut Historical Society.

25   Charles Thomson to John Langdon, April 14, 1789, Langdon-Elwyn Papers, New Hampshire Historical Society.

26   Samuel A. Otis to Nathan Dane, March 28, 1789, Dane Papers, Library of Congress; Otis to Jonathan Dayton, April 9, 1789, Smith Collection, Morristown National Military Park.

27   James Kent to Elizabeth Hamilton, December 2, 1832, Hamilton-McLane Papers, Library of Congress.

28   Kenneth R. Bowling and Helen E. Veit, eds., *The Diary of William Maclay and Other Notes on Senate Debates*, Volume 9 of the *Documentary History of the First Federal Congress* (hereinafter *DHFFC*), p. 5.

29   Fisher Ames to George Richards Minot, July 8-9, 1789, *Works of Ames* 1:61.

30   Charlene Bangs Bickford and Helen E. Veit, eds., *Legislative Histories*, Volumes 4-6 of the *DHFFC*, 6:1844-45.

31   University of Pennsylvania to George Washington, April 20, 1789, Washington Papers, Library of Congress.

32   John Armstrong, Jr., to Horatio Gates, April 7, 1789, Gates Papers, New York Public Library.

33   *Diary of Maclay*, *DHFFC* 9:13.

34   Linda Grant DePauw, Charlene Bangs Bickford, and LaVonne Marlene Siegel, eds., *Senate Legislative Journal*, Volume 1 of the *DHFFC*, p. 31.

35   *Diary of Maclay*, *DHFFC* 9:4.

36   *Senate Legislative Journal*, *DHFFC* 1:45.

37   John Adams to Benjamin Rush, July 24, 1789, Adams Family Manuscript Trust, Massachusetts Historical Society.

38   John Page to St. George Tucker, February 25, 1790, Tucker-Coleman Papers, Swem Library, William and Mary College.

39   *Diary of Maclay*, DHFFC 9:33.

40   Thomas Lloyd, *The Congressional Register* (4 vols., New York, 1789-90), 1:299.

41   *Diary of Maclay*, DHFFC 9:388.

42   William L. Smith to [Edward Rutledge], August 9, 1789, W. L. Smith Papers, South Carolina Historical Society.

43   *Congressional Register* 1:354.

44   *Congressional Register* 1:557.

45   *Congressional Register* 1:531.

46   *Congressional Register* 1:473-74.

47   *Daily Advertiser* (New York), June 20, 1789.

48   *Diary of Maclay*, DHFFC 9:111-12.

49   *Diary of Maclay*, DHFFC 9:114-15.

50   John Steele to Joseph Winston, May 22, 1790, Henry Wagstaff, ed., *The Papers of John Steele* (2 vols., Raleigh, N.C., 1924), 1:61.

51   Elbridge Gerry to Samuel Adams, August 7, 1789, Adams Papers, New York Public Library.

52   *Legislative Histories*, DHFFC 6:1975.

53   Petition of Mary Katherine Goddard, January 29, 1789, Senate Records, National Archives.

54   *Legislative Histories*, DHFFC 5:1165.

55   Robert R. Livingston to Oliver Ellsworth, June 26, 1789, Livingston Papers, New-York Historical Society.

56   John P. Kaminski, Gaspare J. Saladino, Richard Leffler, et al., eds., *Commentaries on the Constitution, Public and Private*, Volume 16 of *The Documentary History of the Ratification of the Constitution*, p. 73.

57   *Diary of Maclay*, DHFFC 9:91.

58   Abraham Baldwin to Joel Barlow, June 14, 1789, Baldwin Folder, Yale University Library.

59   Joseph Jones to James Madison, July 3, 1789, *Papers of Madison* 12:276.

60   Fisher Ames to James Lowell, July 28, 1789, Finestone Collection, American Philosophical Society.

61   Paine Wingate to Judge Nathaniel Sargeant, July 18, 1789, Essex Institute.

62   Abiel Foster to Oliver Peabody, September 23, 1789, Chamberlain Collection, Boston Public Library.

63   Robert Morris to Richard Peters, September 13, 1789, Peters Papers, Historical Society of Pennsylvania.

64   Linda Grant DePauw, Charlene Bangs Bickford, and LaVonne Siegel Hauptman, eds., *House of Representatives Journal*, Volume 3 of the DHFFC, p. 550.

65 Wythe Holt, "Federal Courts as the Asylum to Federal Interests," *Egbert Benson: First Chief Judge of the Second Circuit (1801-1802)*, Second Circuit Committee on the Bicentennial of the United States Constitution (New York, 1987).

66 *Senate Legislative Journal*, DHFFC 1:32.

67 *Congressional Register* 2:249.

68 *Legislative Histories*, DHFFC 4:9.

69 Thomas Jefferson to Madison, March 15, 1789, Julian Boyd, ed., *The Papers of Thomas Jefferson* 14:659.

70 *Legislative Histories*, DHFFC 6:1858.

71 Robert Morris to Mary Morris, September 9, 1789, Morris Papers, Henry E. Huntington Library.

72 John Fenno to Joseph Ward, October 10, 1789, Ward Papers, Chicago Historical Society.

73 William Neilson to John Chaloner, February 17, 1790, Chaloner Papers, Clements Library.

74 Robert Morris to Gouverneur Morris, October 31, 1790, Jared Sparks, *Life of Gouverneur Morris* (3 vols., Boston, 1832), 3:18.

75 Theodorick Bland to St. George Tucker, March 6, 1790, Tucker-Coleman Papers, Swem Library, College of William and Mary.

76 William Maclay to Benjamin Rush, April 12, 1790, Rush Papers, Library of Congress.

77 *Diary of Maclay*, DHFFC 9:241-42.

78 *Papers of Madison* 13:137.

79 Memorial of the Pennsylvania Society for the Abolition of Slavery, February 3, 1790, Senate Records, National Archives.

80 Thomas Cushing to Benjamin Goodhue, April 17, 1790, Goodhue Papers, New York Society Library.

81 Oliver Wolcott, Sr., to Oliver Wolcott, Jr., April 23, 1790, Wolcott Papers, Connecticut Historical Society.

82 John Adams to Stephen Higginson, March 14, 1790, Adams Family Manuscript Trust, Massachusetts Historical Society.

83 *New York Journal*, July 16, 1790.

84 George Clymer to Benjamin Rush, [June] 1789, Bancroft Transcripts, New York Public Library.

85 *Legislative Histories*, DHFFC 4:591-92.

86 Hector St. John de Crevecoeur to William Short, October 7, 1790, Short Papers, Library of Congress.

87 John Rutledge to William Short, March 30, 1791, Short Papers, Library of Congress.

88 Fisher Ames to George Richards Minot, February 17, 1791, *Works of Ames* 1:96.

89   Fisher Ames to Rufus Putnam, February 22, 1791, Putnam Papers, Marietta College.

90   Elias Boudinot to [John Caldwell?], May 17, 1790, Boudinot Papers, Rutgers University.

91   George Clymer to Benjamin Rush, August 7, 1789, Courtesy of Richard H. Kohn, George M. Curtis, III, and Kenneth R. Bowling. A copy is at the Historical Society of Pennsylvania.

92   Samuel H. Parsons to Oliver Ellsworth, May 20, 1789, Parsons Papers, Library of Congress.

93   Arthur Campbell to John Brown, May 1789, Filson Club.

94   *Legislative Histories, DHFFC* 5:1005.

95   *Diary of Maclay, DHFFC* 9:245-46.

96   "C. to Mr. Bache," *General Advertiser* (Philadelphia), January 20, 1791.

97   Paine Wingate to Nathaniel Peabody, February 4, 1791, Peabody Papers, New Hampshire Historical Society.

98   Lacassagne to John Holker, January 13, 1791, Holker Papers, Library of Congress.

99   Nicholas Gilman to Josiah Bartlett, February 6, 1791, Bartlett Papers, Dartmouth College.

100 *Diary of Maclay, DHFFC* 9:130.

101 Allyn Mather to Ebenezer Bernard, July 22 1790, Mather-Bernard Letters, Connecticut Historical Society.

102 Linda Grant DePauw, Charlene Bangs Bickford, and LaVonne Marlene Siegel, eds., *Senate Executive Journal and Related Documents*, Volume 2 of the *DHFFC*, p. 65.

103 Ibid., pp. 451-52.

104 Ibid., pp. 116.

105 *Diary of Maclay, DHFFC* 9:382.

106 *Senate Executive Journal, DHFFC* 2:447.

107 James Madison to Edmund Randolph, March 1, 1789, *Papers of Madison* 11:453.

108 Paine Wingate to Jeremy Belknap, July 6, 1789, Massachusetts Historical Society *Collections*, ser. 6, 4:434

109 William L. Smith to Gabriel Manigault, June 7, 1789, *American Historical Review* 14:767-77.

110 Fisher Ames to George Richards Minot, July, 8, 1789, *Works of Ames* 1:61.

111 Fisher Ames to William Tudor, July 12, 1789, Massachusetts Historical Society *Collections*, ser. 2, 8:319.

112 Fisher Ames to George Richards Minot, July 8-9, 1789, *Works of Ames* 1:62-63.

113 William Grayson to Patrick Henry, September 29, 1789, Henry Papers, Library of Congress.

114 James Madison to Alexander Hamilton, November 19, 1789, *Papers of Madison* 12:451.

115 Theodore Sedgwick to Pamela Sedgwick, March 4, 1790, Sedgwick Papers, Massachusetts Historical Society.

116 Richard Henry Lee to Patrick Henry, June 10, 1790, William Wirt Henry, *Patrick Henry: Life, Correspondence and Speeches* (3 vols., New York, 1891), 3:421.

117 William Few to Governor Edward Telfair, January 15, 1791, Telemon Cuyler Collection, University of Georgia.

118 John Trumbull to John Adams, February. 5, 1791, Adams Family Manuscript Trust, Massachusetts Historical Society.

119 Thomas Jefferson to Robert R. Livingston, February 4, 1791, *Papers of Jefferson* 19:241.

120 Jeremy Belknap to John Wentworth, March 21, 1791, Massachusetts Historical Society *Collections*, ser. 6, 4:484.

121 *Columbian Centinel* (Boston), November 27, 1790.

122 Alexander White to unknown, February 27, 1791, Charles Francis Jenkins Collection, Historical Society of Pennsylvania.

123 Joseph Stanton to Arthur Fenner, February 17, 1791, Rhode Island State Archives.

124 John Trumbull to John Adams, March 20, 1791, Adams Family Manuscript Trust, Massachusetts Historical Society.

Members of the Senate

Bassett, Richard — Delaware, Dover

Butler, Pierce — South Carolina, Prince William Parish

Carroll, Charles — Maryland, Annapolis

Dalton, Tristram — Massachusetts, Newburyport

Dickinson, Philemon — New Jersey, Trenton
(took his seat on December 6, 1790, after being elected to fill the vacancy caused by the resignation of William Paterson)

Ellsworth, Oliver — Connecticut, Hartford

Elmer, Jonathan — New Jersey, Bridgeton

Few, William — Georgia, Augusta

Foster, Theodore — Rhode Island, Providence

Grayson, William — Virginia, Dumfries
(died March 12, 1790)

Gunn, James — Georgia, Savannah

Hawkins, Benjamin — North Carolina, Halifax

Henry, John — Maryland, Dorchester Co.

Izard, Ralph — South Carolina, St. James, Goose Creek

Johnson, William Samuel — Connecticut, Stratford

Johnston, Samuel — North Carolina, Edenton

King, Rufus — New York, New York City

Langdon, John — New Hampshire, Portsmouth

Lee, Richard Henry — Virginia, Westmoreland Co.

Maclay, William — Pennsylvania, Sunbury

Monroe, James — Virginia, Albemarle Co.
(took his seat on December 6, 1790, after being elected to fill the vacancy caused by the death of William Grayson)

Morris, Robert — Pennsylvania, Philadelphia

Paterson, William — New Jersey, New Brunswick
(resigned on November 13, 1790, after being elected governor of New Jersey)

Read, George — Delaware, New Castle

Schuyler, Philip — New York, Albany

Stanton, Joseph, Jr.	Rhode Island, Charlestown
Strong, Caleb	Massachusetts, Northampton
Walker, John	Virginia, Albemarle Co.
(appointed to fill the vacancy caused by the death of William Grayson; served from March 31 through November 9, 1790)	
Wingate, Paine	New Hampshire, Stratham

Members of the House of Representatives

*indicates members elected at large

Ames, Fisher	Massachusetts, Dedham
Ashe, John Baptista	North Carolina, Halifax
Baldwin, Abraham	Georgia, Augusta
Benson, Egbert	New York, Red Hook
Bland, Theodorick (died June 1, 1790)	Virginia, Prince George Co.
Bloodworth, Timothy	North Carolina, Wilmington
Boudinot, Elias*	New Jersey, Elizabethtown
Bourn, Benjamin*	Rhode Island, Providence
Brown, John	Virginia, Frankfort, Ky.
Burke, Aedanus	South Carolina, Charleston
Cadwalader, Lambert*	New Jersey, Trenton
Carroll, Daniel	Maryland, Montgomery Co.
Clymer, George*	Pennsylvania, Philadelphia
Coles, Isaac	Virginia, Halifax Co.
Contee, Benjamin	Maryland, Prince Georges Co.
Fitzsimons, Thomas*	Pennsylvania, Philadelphia
Floyd, William	New York, Brookhaven
Foster, Abiel*	New Hampshire, Canterbury
Gale, George	Maryland, Somerset Co.
Gerry, Elbridge	Massachusetts, Cambridge

Giles, William B. (took his seat on December 7, 1790, after being elected to fill the vacancy caused by the death of Theodorick Bland)	Virginia, Petersburg
Gilman, Nicholas*	New Hampshire, Exeter
Goodhue, Benjamin	Massachusetts, Salem
Griffin, Samuel	Virginia, Richmond Co.
Grout, Jonathan	Massachusetts, Petersham
Hartley, Thomas*	Pennsylvania, York
Hathorn, John	New York, Warwick
Hiester, Daniel, Jr.*	Pennsylvania, Montgomery Co.
Huger, Daniel	South Carolina, Georgetown
Huntington, Benjamin*	Connecticut, Norwich
Jackson, James	Georgia, Savannah
Laurance, John	New York, New York City
Lee, Richard Bland	Virginia, Loudoun Co.
Leonard, George	Massachusetts, Norton
Livermore, Samuel*	New Hampshire, Holderness
Madison, James, Jr.	Virginia, Orange Co.
Mathews, George	Georgia, Washington
Moore, Andrew	Virginia, Rockbridge Co.
Muhlenberg, Frederick A.*	Pennsylvania, Montgomery Co.
Muhlenberg, Peter*	Pennsylvania, Montgomery Co.
Page, John	Virginia, Gloucester Co.
Parker, Josiah	Virginia, Isle of Wight Co.
Partridge, George	Massachusetts, Duxbury
Schureman, James*	New Jersey, New Brunswick
Scott, Thomas*	Pennsylvania, Westmoreland Co.
Sedgwick, Theodore	Massachusetts, Stockbridge
Seney, Joshua	Maryland, Queen Annes Co.
Sevier, John	North Carolina, Knoxville, Tenn.
Sherman, Roger*	Connecticut, New Haven
Silvester, Peter	New York, Kinderhook
Sinnickson, Thomas*	New Jersey, Salem

Smith, William	Maryland, Baltimore
Smith, William L.	South Carolina, Charleston
Steele, John	North Carolina, Salisbury
Stone, Michael Jenifer	Maryland, Port Tobacco
Sturges, Jonathan	Connecticut, Fairfield
Sumter, Thomas	South Carolina, Statesburg
Thatcher, George	Massachusetts, Biddeford, Me.
Trumbull, Jonathan*	Connecticut, Lebanon
Tucker, Thomas Tudor	South Carolina, Charleston
Van Rensselaer, Jeremiah	New York, Albany
Vining, John*	Delaware, Dover
Wadsworth, Jeremiah*	Connecticut, Hartford
White, Alexander	Virginia, Winchester
Williamson, Hugh	North Carolina, Edenton
Wynkoop, Henry*	Pennsylvania, Bucks Co.

Index

Adams, John: casts deciding vote, 41; on dissolution of the Union, 68; election, 16, 23–24; letters to, 93, 100; residence, 36; role as vice president, 88; satirized, 28; on titles, 26, 28; on western expansion, 77, 78
Adams, John Quincy, 93
Adams, Samuel, 41
Advice and consent, 87
Alcohol, effects on health, 72
Alexandria, Va., 57, 70, 74, 75
Algiers, U.S. hostages in, 86, 87, 90–91
Amendments: *See* Constitution, amendments
American Daily Advertiser, 18
American Geography, 77
American Revolution, 1, 2, 7, 55, 73, 77, 93, 99. *See also* Revolutionary War
Ames, Fisher: on assumption, 65; on capital city, 58; on Congress, 1, 10, 12, 16, 20; district, 5; illus., 92; on Jefferson, 97; on Judiciary Act [S-1], 47; political leader, 97; on political parties, 94; on removal power, 39, 40; on western expansion, 78
Anacostia River, 70, 74
Annapolis, Md., 4
Antifederalists, 2, 4, 10–12, 23, 33, 43, 46, 48, 51, 52, 53, 93, 94, 95, 97
Appropriations, 34, 35, 81, 82, 91
Army, 3, 52, 60, 78, 80, 81, 82, 83–84, 100. *See also* Military policy; Militia; Conscientious objection
Articles of Confederation, 2–3, 4, 7, 9, 29, 41, 45, 56, 62
Assumption of state debts, 3, 31, 58, 62, 64–72, 88, 95–96
Attorney General, 43, 49, 73

Balance of powers, 5, 15, 41, 43, 49

Baldwin, Abraham, 10–12, 46–47
Baltimore, Md., 4, 43, 57, 70
Bank, national, 3, 64, 73
Bank Bill [S-15], 73
Bankson, Benjamin, 46
Barbary States, 90–91
Beckley, John, 16–17
Belknap, Jeremy, 1, 6, 99
Benson, Egbert, 49
Bill of Rights. *See* Constitution, amendments
Bland, Theodorick, 39, 65
Board of Treasury, 37
Boudinot, Elias: on assumption, 66; on executive departments, 38; on New York City, 10; on western expansion, 78–80
Bourn, Sylvanus, 16
Bowery, The, 9
Brown, Andrew, 18
"Brutus," 46
Bryan, Samuel, 61
Budget, federal, 35
Burke, Aedanus, 18, 48, 53, 61

Cabinet, 52
Capital city, 3, 4, 5, 16, 48, 52, 55–59, 65–72, 74, 94–95, 96
Capitol, U.S., 17, 46
Carlisle, Pa., 57
Carmichael, William, 37
Carroll, Charles, 69, 70, 71, 74
Carroll, Daniel, 69, 70, 71, 72
Cartoons, 25, 70, 73
Census, 5, 38
Charleston, S.C., 4–5
Checks and balances, 38
Cherokee Indians, 88
Chesapeake Bay, 33
Chester, Pa., 24

Chickasaw Indians, 88
Chocktaw Indians, 88
Clinton, George, 25
Clymer, George: on assumption, 65; on
    excise, 72; illus., 76; on western
    expansion, 79, 80
Coast Guard, 33
Coasting Act [HR-16], 30, 33
Collection Act [HR-11], 30, 32–33
Columbia, Pa., 57
Commerce, 2, 31, 62, 90
Compromise of 1790, 67–75, 96
Consular Convention of 1788, 87
Congress, Confederation, 3, 4, 6, 7, 9,
    10–12, 15, 16, 17, 29, 35, 37, 38, 55–56,
    62, 84–85, 93
Congress, Continental, 2, 3, 4, 10–12, 17,
    60, 71, 93
Congress, first federal: adjournment, 67,
    94; agenda, 13; committee to meet
    Washington, 22, 23; conference
    committees, 31–32; convening, 4, 9,
    10–12, 18; elections, 4–5, 51, 52, 53, 93;
    evaluated, 99–100; expectations for, 1,
    5, 6, 18; expenses, 100; joint rules, 21;
    lack of quorum, 10, 15–16, 31; members
    described, 12–13; organization, 15–21,
    58, 100; petitions, 6, 31, 33, 35, 38, 43,
    62, 63, 68, 72, 82–83, 84; precedents,
    21; 31, 88; quorum, 15–16; salaries, 21;
    subcommittees, 46. See also House of
    Representatives; Senate
Congress, second federal, 100
Congress, third, 5
Congress Hall, 73, 74
Congressional Register, 18
Connecticut, 6, 54; electors, 23; federal
    election, 4; governor, 16
Conococheague Creek, 70
Conscientious objection, 54, 82
Constituent services, 6
Constitution, 72, 81; amendments, xii, 3,
    4, 17, 26, 29, 46, 48, 49, 50–54, 94, 95;
    as revolution, 3–4, 53, 61, 62, 67, 72;
    and assumption, 65; interpretation, 1,
    5–6, 37, 38–41, 43, 48, 68, 72, 73, 74,
    96–97; provisions, 3, 5, 20, 23, 29, 33,
    45, 82, 85, 87; ratification, 1, 3–4, 7, 9,
    17, 33, 45–46, 51, 53, 93, 95, 97
Constitutional Convention. See Federal
    Convention
Copyrights, 38
Counterfeiting, 49
Courts. See Judicial branch; Judiciary Act
    [S-1]
Creek Indians, 81, 82, 88, 90

Crevecoeur, Hector St. John de, 72
Crimes, federal, 49
Cumberland Gazette (Portland, Maine), 9

Debt: federal, 6, 29, 31, 58, 59, 60–72,
    95; private, 48; state, 58, 62. See also
    Assumption of state debts
Declaration of Independence, 2, 53, 97
Delaware, 68
Delaware River, 55
Democracy, 3, 94
Democratic-Republican Party, 97
Domestic department, 38
Dunlap, John, 18
Duties on Distilled Spirits Act [HR-110],
    31, 33, 71–72

Eastern states. See New England States
Economy, national, 3
Elections, first federal, 4–5, 51, 52, 53, 93
Electors, presidential, 4, 16, 23
Ellsworth, Oliver: on assumption, 66; in
    Confederation Congress, 3; illus., 47;
    on Judiciary Act [S-1], 43, 46–47; on
    public credit, 62; on removal power,
    40; on western expansion, 80
Empire, American, 23, 68, 77–80, 85, 99
Excise, 31, 52, 64, 71–72
Executive branch, 3, 16, 29, 51, 52, 69,
    73, 94; departments, 37–43; lobbying
    by, 68; role of, 2, 23–28; and western
    expansion, 78, 80–84

Federal Convention, 3, 10–12, 23, 45, 51,
    61, 62, 68, 84, 93
Federal Gazette, 18
Federal Hall, 9–12, 25, 56, 70, 73; illus.,
    8
Federalism, 1–4, 5, 15, 25, 33, 41, 51, 52,
    57, 61–62, 82, 93, 94, 95–97
Federalists, 3–4, 10–12, 18, 23, 33, 41, 48,
    52, 53, 57, 93, 94, 95, 97
Fenno, John, 18, 62, 94
Few, William, 6, 96–97
Fines, 35
Fitzsimons, Thomas: on assumption, 65,
    66; conflict of interest, 30; on impost
    debate, 31; on Northwest Territory, 84
Florida, 88
Foreign Affairs Act [HR-8], 38, 40
Foreign policy, 31, 87–91
Foster, Abiel, 45, 48
Fourteenth Amendment, 54
France, 31, 64, 87, 90
Franklin, Benjamin, 68, 77

Frederick, Md., 69
Funding Act [HR-63], 1, 65–72, 95

Gale, George, 70, 71
Garland, George, 60
Gazette of the United States, 5, 18, 94
George III, 1, 2
Georgetown, Md., 55, 57, 70
Georgia, 54, 81, 82, 90
Germantown, Pa., 57, 58
Gerry, Elbridge: on amendments to
    Constitution, 51; on assumption,
    65–66; on Treasury department, 41, 94
Gilman, Nicholas, 83
Goddard, Mary Katherine, 43
Goodhue, Benjamin, 57, 68
Grayson, William: on amendments to
    Constitution, 50; on capital city, 56,
    95; on Collection Act [HR-11], 32–33;
    on Senate's executive role, 41
Great Britain: and American Revolution,
    30, 88, 99; boundary with U.S., 77–78,
    90; creditors, 48; Parliament, 1, 2, 18,
    41; trade, 31, 90
Greenwich Village, 9, 13

Hamilton, Alexander: bank proposal,
    73–74; character, 62–64; compromise
    of 1790, 68–71; in Confederation
    Congress, 3, 62; drafts legislation, 42;
    excise proposal, 71–72; on House
    debate, 18; on presidential election,
    23–24; report on public credit, 35, 58,
    59, 61–66, 95. *See also* Treasury,
    Secretary of
Harpers Ferry, W.Va., 70
Henry, Patrick, 41, 50, 95
History, use of, 18, 55, 80
Hospitals and Harbors Bill [HR-22],
    33–35
Hostage crisis, 90–91
House of Representatives: chamber, 9;
    clerk, 16–17, 21; committee of the
    whole, 20; conflict of interest, 29–30;
    elections, 4–5; offices, 9; organization,
    16, 30; pay, 21; quorum, 16; records, 17;
    reporting of debates, 17–18; rules, 20;
    size of districts, 5; Speaker, 16. *See also*
    Congress, first federal; Elections, first
    federal
Hudson River, 9, 13, 78, 84
Humphreys, David, 24, 25, 26, 88

Impeachment, 2, 38–39, 40
Implied powers, 40, 41, 52, 72

Impost duties, 15, 16, 29–32, 53, 93
Inaugural address, 25–26, 80
Independence Hall, 73
Indians, 35, 38, 77, 81–84, 87, 88, 90–91
Inspection Act [HR-48], 33
Interstate commerce, 2
Iredell, James, 5

Jackson, James: on amendments to
    Constitution, xii; district, 5; on removal
    power, 40; on sectionalism, 94
Jay, John, 23, 37, 87
Jefferson, Thomas: ambassador, 87; on
    amendments to Constitution, 52, 54;
    arrives in New York City, 37; on bank
    bill, 73–74; compromise of 1790,
    68–69; letters to, 5, 55; on political
    parties, 97. *See also* State, Secretary of
Judicial branch, 2, 3, 16, 35, 45–49, 51,
    94; constitutional amendments, 51, 52;
    role, 54; salaries, 48
Judicial review, 45, 46, 48
Judiciary Act [S-1], 43, 44, 46–49

Kent, James, 18
Kentucky, 80, 85
King, Rufus, 70
Knox, Henry, 37, 67. *See also* War,
    Secretary of

Lake Erie, 82
Lancaster, Pa., 4, 57
Lands, western, 61, 77, 78, 80, 84, 100
Langdon, John, 24
Laurance, John, 32
Lee, Henry, 67
Lee, Richard Bland, 57, 70, 71, 72
Lee, Richard Henry, 96; on Collection
    Act [HR-11], 32–33; takes seat, 16; on
    titles, 26
Lee, Robert E., 67
Legislative supremacy, 3, 37, 94
L'Enfant, Pierre, 9, 84
Liability of Shipowners Bill [HR-107], 35
Lighthouses Act [HR-12], 33
Livermore, Samuel, 48
Livingston, Robert R., 43, 97
Lloyd, Thomas, 18, 19
Lobbying, 78, 80, 84
Long Island, 13
Luzerne, Marquis de la, 67

McGillivray, Alexander, 88
Maclay, William, 28; on assumption, 65,
    88; on Collection Act [HR-11], 33; on

Congress, 6, 16, 20, 21; diary, 18, 89; on diplomacy, 90; illus., 20; on Judiciary Act [S-1], 46; on military policy, 82; on removal power, 40, 41; on revenue, 29–30; on Senate's executive role, 88; on titles, 26; on Washington, 25

Madison, James, 77; on adjournment, 67; on amendments to Constitution, 50–54; on bank, 73; on capital city, 56, 57, 58, 94–95; on census, 5; on Collection Act [HR-11], 33; on compromise of 1790, 67, 69, 71, 72; in Confederation Congress, 3; on Congress, 12, 15; on congressional pay, 21; election, 4; on executive departments, 38; on federalism, 95; illus., 96; on impost duties, 30, 31; on interpretation of Constitution, 5, 38, 40, 73; on Judiciary Act [S-1], 47, 48; on political parties, 93, 95–97; presidential advisor, 26; on public credit, 62, 64, 65; on removal power, 40; on revenue, 29; on western expansion, 78

Madison, James, Sr., 15
Maine, 33, 90
Manhattan Island, 9, 13
Manufacturing, 29, 31
Marietta, Ohio, 78, 80
Maryland, 6, 68, 74; delegation, 70; electors, 24; federal election, 4; governor, 43
Mason, George, 51, 54
Massachusetts, 54, 62, 65; boundary, 90; delegation, 65–66, 70, 71; districts, 5; federal election, 4; House of Representatives, 17
Merchant Seamen Act [HR-61], 33
Middle States, 6, 31, 58, 94
Military Establishment Act [HR-50a], 81–82
Military Establishment Bill [HR-126A], 84
Military exemptions, 54, 82
Military policy, 52, 77, 81–84, 91
Militia, 52, 81–83, 99
Mint, 99
Molasses, 30–31, 72
Monarchy, 23, 25, 26, 28, 39
Monroe, James, 4
Moore, Stephen, 84
Morris, Gouverneur, 37, 72, 85, 90
Morris, Robert, 15, 24; on capital city, 57, 58, 70, 73; on Congress, 6; on Judiciary Act [S-1], 48; on public credit, 65; satirized, 73; on Senate's

executive role, 88; superintendent of finance, 3, 37, 62, 64
Morse, Jedidiah, 77
Muhlenberg, Frederick Augustus: on capital city, 10; elected Speaker, 16; illus., 14; on political parties, 94

Nationalism, 1–2, 3, 23
Navy, 80
Necessary and proper clause, 39–40, 97
Netherlands, The, 64, 65
New England States, 6, 68; delegation, 58, 68, 69, 70; interests, 30, 31, 55, 72, 77, 78, 94
New Hampshire, 4
New Jersey, 13, 57, 68; federal election, 4, 5
New York City: capital city, 4, 5, 9, 10, 55–58, 68, 70, 71, 73; celebrations, 10, 24–25; illus., 30; lobbying by, 56, 58; welcomes Washington, 22, 24–25
New York *Morning Post* , 11
New York Society Library, 10
New York State, 6, 29, 55, 67, 68, 97; chancellor, 43; delegation, 58, 68; federal election, 4, 23–24; governor, 25, 88; legislature, 23; ratifying convention, 2, 17; senators, 58
North Carolina, 5, 58
North Carolina Act [HR-36], 33
Northern States, 64. *See also* Sectionalism
Northwest Territory, 78, 81, 84–85, 90
Nova Scotia, 90

Oath Act [HR-1], 1–2
O'Bryan, Richard, 87, 90–91
Officeholders, 6, 33, 38
Ohio Company, 78
Ohio River, 70
Osgood, Samuel, 5
Otis, Samuel Allyne, 17, 20

"Pacificus," 51
Page, John, 28
Pardons, 52
Patents, 10, 38
Paterson, William, 46
Patronage, 33
Peabody, Oliver, 45
Pennsylvania, 6; Assembly, 16; capital city in, 55, 56, 57, 68; delegation, 57, 58, 68, 69, 70; federal election, 4; petition of public creditors, 62, 63; ratifying convention, 16; State House, 73
Pensions for veterans, 100

People, power from, 53
Peters, Richard, 55
Petitions. *See* Congress, first federal
Philadelphia: capital city, 4, 5, 10, 56–59,
     70, 71, 73; College of Physicians, 72;
     reception for Washington, 24
Pickering, Timothy, 60
Political cartoons, 25, 70, 73
Political parties, 10–12, 93–97
Political satire, 25, 28, 82–83
Portland Head Lighthouse Act [HR-97],
     33
Postmaster General, 43
Post Office, 43, 99
Potomac River, 33, 55, 57, 58, 65–72, 73,
     75, 94, 96, 97
Presidency Act [HR-104], 97
President, 3, 23–28, 85; on capital city,
     55, 57–58, 71, 73, 74; check on
     judiciary, 51; inauguration, 10, 22,
     25–26, 52, 80; powers, 39–41, 52;
     residence, 13, 25, 88; salary, 26; and
     senate, 87–91; succession, 97, 100;
     term of office, 52; title, 23, 26–28, 78;
     on tonnage duties, 90; veto, 57–58, 71,
     73, 74–75; Washington's role as, 23,
     40, 41; on western expansion, 80–83.
     See also Executive branch
Public credit, 29, 58, 59, 61–66, 71–72,
     95
Public opinion, 82–83
Punishment of Crimes Act [S-6], 48–49
Putnam, Rufus, 78

Quakers, 68, 82
Quorum, lack of, 10, 15–16

Ramsay, David, 5
Randolph, Edmund, 49, 73
Reading, Pa., 57
Records, federal, 38, 46
Republicanism, 82, 94, 95
Reserved powers, 2, 52
Residence Act [S-12], 58–59. *See also*
     Capital city
Revenue, federal, 2, 3, 15–16, 26, 29–35,
     48, 51, 52, 61, 62, 64, 65, 71, 72, 78,
     90, 93, 94, 100
Revolutionary War, 2, 3, 6, 9, 29, 31, 37,
     61, 71, 82, 84, 88
Rhode Island, 29, 58, 78
Rhode Island Act [HR-71], 33
Richmond, Va., 7
Richmond Hill, N.Y., 36
Rum, 72

Rush, Benjamin, 72, 79

St. Clair, Arthur, 81
Salaries, 21, 26, 48
Science and technology, 38
Scott, Thomas, 80
Seat of Government Bill [HR-25], 57, 58.
     See also Capital city
Sectionalism, 1, 6–7, 10, 12, 17, 29, 30–31,
     48, 51, 55–59, 65, 67–75, 77, 78, 85,
     93–97, 99–100
Sedgwick, Theodore: on assumption, 65;
     district, 5; on Judiciary Act [S-1], 48;
     on Madison, 95; on removal power, 39
Senate: chamber, 10, 25; closed doors, 17,
     18; election, 4; executive role, 39,
     40–41, 87–91; filibuster, 58; journal,
     20; offices, 10; organization, 16, 17; pay,
     21; president pro tempore, 24; quorum,
     15; records, 17; removal of executive
     officers, 39–41; rules, 20–21; secretary,
     17, 20, 21; on titles, 23, 26–28. *See also*
     Congress, first federal
Separation of powers, 38, 41, 43, 45, 51,
     54
Settlement of accounts, 71
Sherman, Roger, 29, 53
Ship of state metaphor, xii, 4, 53, 99
Shipping, 31
Sinking fund, 71
Slavery, 6, 39, 58, 68, 72, 90–91, 100
Smith, William Loughton (S.C.): election,
     5; on removal power, 38–39, 40; on
     sectionalism, 94
South Carolina, 39; debt, 62, 65;
     delegation, 33, 58, 68; electors, 24;
     federal election, 4–5
Southern States, 82. *See also* Sectionalism
Spain, 77–78, 80, 88
Sparks, Jared, 26
Speculation, 64–65
Stamp Act (1765), 1
Stanton, Joseph, 99–100
State, Secretary of, 17, 38. *See also*
     Jefferson, Thomas
States: admission of new, 77, 85;
     assumption of federal debt, 61–62;
     boundaries, 33; courts, 51;
     infringement of rights by, 54; officials
     of, 1–2. *See also* Northwest Territory
States' rights, 1–2, 33, 45, 46, 51, 62, 65,
     93, 95, 96–97
Stephen, Adam, 77
Strong, Caleb, 46
Stuart, David, 57–58
Supremacy clause, 3, 4, 52

Susquehanna River, 56, 57, 94, 95
Swift, Jonathan, 53

Tariff. *See* Impost duties
Taxes, 3, 52, 61, 100. *See also* Revenue
Tea, 30
Thatcher, George, 5, 10
Thomson, Charles, 16, 17, 20, 24, 38
Titles, 23, 26–28, 78
Tonnage duties, 30, 31–32, 90
Treason, 49
Treasury, Secretary of, 37, 41–43, 84, 94.
    See also Hamilton, Alexander
Treasury Act [HR-9], 38, 42, 94
Treaties of Fort Harmar, 87
Treaty of New York (1790), 88–90
Treaty of Paris (1783), 3, 48
Trenton, N.J., 55, 57
Troops Act [HR-27], 81
Trumbull, John, 10, 96, 100
Tucker, St. George, 23
Tucker, Thomas Tudor, 23, 28, 48
Tudor, William, 1

Union, dissolution of, 1, 7, 48, 57, 65,
    67, 68, 73, 78, 80
University of Pennsylvania, 24

Vermont, 85
Veto. *See* President, veto
Vice President, 23. *See* Adams, John
Vincennes, Ill., 84
Virginia, 4, 6, 55; Declaration of Rights,
    54; on dissolution of the Union, 67,
    68; federal election, 4; legislature, 17,
    96; ratification of Constitution, 31, 95;
    ratifies Bill of Rights, 54; senators,
    10–12, 18

Wabash Indians, 81, 82, 83
Wadsworth, Jeremiah, 66
War, Secretary of, 80–81, 82, 83, 87, 88
War Department Act [HR-7], 38
War of 1812, 17
Warren, Charles, 46
Washington, D.C. *See* Capital city; Seat of
    Government Bill [HR-25]; Residence
    Act [S-12]
Washington, George, 77; on amendments
    to Constitution, 52; commander in
    chief of Continental army, 3, 23; on
    compromise of 1790, 67, 71, 73, 74; on
    Congress, 12; election, 16, 17, 23, 24;
    inaugural address, 25–26, 80; journey
    to New York City, 24; respect for,
    24–25, 41; satirized, 25; welcome in
    New York City, 22, 24–25. *See also*
    President
Ways and Means Act [HR-83], 31
Webster, Noah, 51
Western expansion, 77–85
West Indies, 90
West Point, 84
Whiskey Rebellion, 72
White, Alexander, 69–70, 71, 72, 99
White Eyes, George M., 35
Williamsport, Md., 70
Wingate, Paine: on Congress, 6, 70; on
    Judiciary Act [S-1], 47–48; on Indian
    policy, 83; on sectionalism, 93
Wolcott, Oliver, 29
Women, 43, 82–83
Wright's Ferry, Pa., 57

York, Pa., 57
Yorktown, battle of, 2